Harvard
Business
Review

ON
CUSTOMER RELATIONSHIP
MANAGEMENT

THE HARVARD BUSINESS REVIEW PAPERBACK SERIES

The series is designed to bring today's managers and professionals the fundamental information they need to stay competitive in a fast-moving world. From the preeminent thinkers whose work has defined an entire field to the rising stars who will redefine the way we think about business, here are the leading minds and landmark ideas that have established the *Harvard Business Review* as required reading for ambitious businesspeople in organizations around the globe.

Other books in the series:

Other books in the series (continued):

Harvard Business Review

ON

CUSTOMER RELATIONSHIP MANAGEMENT

The *Harvard Business Review* articles in this collection are available as
individual reprints. Discounts apply to quantity purchases. For information and ordering, please contact Customer Service, Harvard Business
School Publishing, Boston, MA 02163. Telephone: (617) 783-7500 or
(800) 988-0886, 8 A.M. to 6 P.M. Eastern Time, Monday through Friday.
Fax: (617) 783-7555, 24 hours a day. E-mail: custserv@hbsp.harvard.edu

Library of Congress Cataloging-in-Publication Data
Harvard business review on customer relationship management.
    p.   cm. — (A Harvard business review paperback)
    Includes bibliographical references and index.
    ISBN 1-57851-699-4 (alk. paper)
    1. Customer relations—Management. I. Title: Customer relation-
ship management. II. Harvard Business School Press. III. Harvard
business review. IV. Harvard business review paperback series.
HF5414.5 .H37   2002
658.8′12—dc21   2001039850
                                                            CIP

*The paper used in this publication meets the requirements of the Ameri-
can National Standard for Permanence of Paper for Publications and
Documents in Libraries and Archives Z39.48-1992.*

Contents

Harvard Business Review

ON

CUSTOMER RELATIONSHIP MANAGEMENT

Co-opting Customer Competence

C.K. PRAHALAD AND

VENKATRAM RAMASWAMY

Executive Summary

MAJOR BUSINESS TRENDS such as deregulation, globalization, technological convergence, and the rapid evolution of the Internet have transformed the roles that companies play in their dealings with other companies. Business practitioners and scholars talk about alliances, networks, and collaboration among companies, But managers and researchers have largely ignored the agent that is most dramatically transforming the industrial systems as we know it: the consumer.

In a market in which technology-enabled consumers can now engage themselves in an active dialogue with manufacturers—a dialogue that customers can control—companies have to recognize that the customer is becoming a partner in creating value. In this article, authors C.K. Prahalad and Venkatram Ramaswamy demonstrate how the shifting role of the consumer affects the notion of a company's core competencies. Where previously, business learned to draw on competencies and resources of their business partners and suppliers to compete effectively, they must now include consumers as a part of the extended enterprise, the authors say.

Harnessing those customer competencies won't be easy. At a minimum, managers must come to grips with four fundamental realities in co-opting customer competence: they have to engage their customers in an active, explicit, and ongoing dialogue; mobilize communities of customers; manager customer diversity; and engage customers in cocreating personalized experiences.

Companies will also need to revise some of the traditional mechanisms of the marketplace—pricing and billing systems, for instance—to account for their customers' new role.

BUSINESS COMPETITION used to be a lot like traditional theater: On stage, the actors had clearly defined roles, and the customers paid for their tickets, sat back, and watched passively. In business, companies, distributors, and suppliers understood and adhered to their well-defined roles in a corporate relationship. Now the scene has changed, and business competition seems more like the experimental theater of the 1960s and 1970s; everyone and anyone can be part of the action.

The shift away from formal, defined roles is already occurring in business-to-business relationships. Major business discontinuities such as deregulation, globalization, technological convergence, and the rapid evolution of the Internet have blurred the roles that companies play in their dealings with other businesses. Consider the relationship between Ford and its main suppliers. Far from being passive providers of materials and parts, Ford's suppliers have become close collaborators in the development of new vehicles. At the same time, however, they compete for value by negotiating the prices for the parts and the materials they supply. Some suppliers are starting to compete directly. For example, Markham, Ontario-based auto-parts giant Magna International has the ambition—and the potential—to assemble automobiles itself.

The story's the same for distributors. For example, Wal-Mart does more than just distribute Procter & Gamble's goods. It shares daily sales information and works with P&G in product warehousing and replenishment to ensure that consumers can always find the goods they want at low prices. In some product categories, however, Wal-Mart competes head-to-head with P&G. For instance, Wal-Mart last year rolled out its own brand of detergent, Sam's American Choice, which competes nationally with P&G's popular Tide brand.

The changing dynamics of business has been the focus of managerial debate the past few years. Practitioners and scholars talk about companies "competing as a family." They talk about alliances, networks, and collaboration among companies. But managers and researchers have largely ignored the consumer, the agent that is most dramatically transforming the industrial system as we know it. (See the exhibit "The Evolution and Transformation of Customers.")

Thanks largely to the Internet, consumers have been increasingly engaging themselves in an active and explicit dialogue with manufacturers of products and services. What's more, that dialogue is no longer being controlled by corporations. Individual consumers can

The Evolution and Transformation of Customers

Customers are stepping out of their traditional roles to become cocreators as well as consumers of value. This table maps their evolution through three stages and along several key dimensions.

	CUSTOMERS AS A PASSIVE AUDIENCE			CUSTOMERS AS ACTIVE PLAYERS
	Persuading predetermined groups of buyers	**Transacting with individual buyers**	**Lifetime bonds with individual customers**	**Customers as cocreators of value**
Time frame	1970s, early 1980s	Late 1980s and early 1990s	1990s	Beyond 2000
Nature of business exchange and role of customer	Customers are seen as passive buyers with a predetermined role of consumption.			Customers are part of the enhanced network; they cocreate and extract business value. They are collaborators, codevelopers, and competitors.
Managerial mind-set	The customer is an average statistic; groups of buyers are predetermined by the company.	The customer is an individual statistic in a transaction.	The customer is a person; cultivate trust and relationships.	The customer is not only an individual but also part of an emergent social and cultural fabric.
Company's interaction with customers, and development of products and services	Traditional market research and inquiries; products and services are created without much feedback.	Shift from selling to helping customers via help desks, call centers, and customer service programs; identify problems from customers, then redesign products and services based on that feedback.	Providing for customers through observation of users; identify solutions from lead users, and reconfigure products and services based on deep understanding of customers.	Customers are codevelopers of personalized experiences. Companies and lead customers have joint roles in education, shaping expectations, and cocreating market acceptance for products and services.
Purpose and flow of communication	Gain access to and target predetermined groups of buyers. One-way communication.	Database marketing; two-way communication.	Relationship marketing; two-way communication and access.	Active dialogue with customers to shape expectations and create buzz. Multilevel access and communication.

address and learn about businesses either on their own or through the collective knowledge of other customers. Consumers can now initiate the dialogue; they have moved out of the audience and onto the stage.

Customers are fundamentally changing the dynamics of the marketplace. The market has become a forum in which consumers play an active role in creating and competing for value. The distinguishing feature of this new marketplace is that consumers become a new source of competence for the corporation. The competence that customers bring is a function of the knowledge and skills they possess, their willingness to learn and experiment, and their ability to engage in an active dialogue.

The concept of competence as a source of competitive advantage originated in studies of the diversified firm.[1] Managers started to conceive of the company as a collection of competencies rather than as a portfolio of business units. In this way, managers were able to identify new business opportunities and find new ways to deploy the company's intellectual assets. Managers eventually came to realize that the corporation could also draw on the competencies of its supply-chain partners. During the last decade, managers have extended the search for competencies even further; they now draw on a broad network of suppliers and distributors. Over time, then, the unit of strategic analysis has moved from the single company, to a family of businesses, and finally to what people call the "extended enterprise," which consists of a central firm supported by a constellation of suppliers. But the recognition that consumers are a source of competence forces managers to cast an even wider net: competence now is a function of the collective knowledge available to the whole system—an enhanced network of traditional suppliers, manufacturers, partners, investors,

and customers. (See the exhibit "The Shifting Locus of
Core Competencies.")

Customers as a Source of Competence

Some industries have already gone further than others in
drawing on the competencies of customers. Consider the
software industry, in which companies have moved from
testing products in usability laboratories to testing them
in customer environments. For example, more than
650,000 customers tested a beta version of Microsoft's
Windows 2000 and shared with the software giant their
ideas for changing some of the product's features. Many
of those customers were even prepared to pay Microsoft
a fee to do this. Working with the beta software helped
many of those customers understand how Windows
2000 could create value for their own businesses. The
beta tests also helped clear the glitches from early versions of the software. The value of the collective R&D
investment by Microsoft's customers in codeveloping
Windows was estimated at more than $500 million
worth of time, effort, and fees.

In Microsoft's case, customers act as product testers
in their native environments. Internetworking giant
Cisco goes even further than that; it gives its customers
open access to its information, resources, and systems
through an on-line service that enables Cisco's customers to engage in a dialogue. In this way, Cisco's customers solve the problems encountered by other customers, and each customer has access to Cisco's
knowledge base and user community. They are engaged
in helping one another.

The notion of the customer as a source of competence
is starting to appear in less obvious industries, too. Take

The Shifting Locus of Core Competencies

	The company	Family/network of companies	Enhanced network
Unit of analysis	The company	The extended enterprise—the company, its suppliers, and its partners	The whole system—the company, its suppliers, its partners, and its customers
Resources	What is available within the company	Access to other companies' competencies and investments	Access to other companies' competencies and investments, as well as customers' competencies and investments of time and effort
Basis for access to competence	Internal company-specific processes	Privileged access to companies within the network	Infrastructure for active ongoing dialogue with diverse customers
Value added of managers	Nurture and build competencies	Manage collaborative partnerships	Harness customer competence, manage personalized experiences, and shape customer expectations
Value creation	Autonomous	Collaborate with partner companies	Collaborate with partner companies and with active customers
Sources of managerial tension	Business-unit autonomy versus leveraging core competencies	Partner is both collaborator and competitor for value	Customer is both collaborator and competitor for value

medicine. Andy Grove, chairman of Intel, in 1995 was diagnosed with prostate cancer. He researched the causes of the disease and, with his doctors, developed a unique treatment plan. Now, you may expect someone like Grove to take his treatment into his own hands, but the point is that he is hardly alone. The availability of medical information on the Internet, in magazines such as *Time*, *Newsweek*, and *Reader's Digest*, on TV, and in local newspapers is helping more and more patients enter into a dialogue with their doctors. The more knowledgeable they become, the more likely these customers are to shape their health care regimen. Doctors may resent the consumer's exercise of his or her knowledge, but they would do well to learn how to co-opt it.

Harnessing the competencies of the consumer is not an easy task. It's complicated enough for a large company like Ford to understand its internal competence base, let alone the competencies of each of its top 100 suppliers. Just imagine how difficult it will be for Ford's managers to understand the competence base of the millions of heterogeneous individuals who are the automaker's customers. But that's the challenge. At a minimum, managers must come to grips with four fundamental realities in harnessing customer competence. They have to engage their customers in an active, explicit, and ongoing dialogue; they have to mobilize communities of customers; they have to manage customer diversity; and they have to cocreate personalized experiences with customers. Let's take a closer look at each task.

ENCOURAGING ACTIVE DIALOGUE

In the new marketplace, companies have to recognize that their dialogue with their customers is a dialogue of equals. Companies no longer have a monopoly on—or even an advantage in—information access. For example, stock prices, market data, and trading information—long the preserve of brokers—are now widely available on the Internet; on-line brokers such as E*Trade and Charles Schwab now boast more than two million regular customers as a result.

But engaging in a dialogue with customers who know what they want requires richer and subtler forms of exchange than many companies are used to. Traditional stockbrokers could talk to customers and, during the exchange, could find out lots of information about them; the conversation had to take place because the customers needed the information that the brokers had. But now these same customers may only want the broker to supply an easy, safe, and reliable execution of their predetermined trades. It becomes critical, therefore, for companies to understand the purpose, meaning, and quality of the dialogue from the customer's perspective. What's more, a dialogue must evolve—or die. Companies are going to have to find ways to process what they learn from customers so they can bring the dialogue forward and keep the consumer's interest.

Progressive Internet companies have adapted best to the new dialogue. That's largely because the Internet has done the most to increase the customer's power as an interlocuter. A good example is Amazon.com. Each time an Amazon customer accesses the company's Web site, the on-line bookseller provides recommendations based not only on the customer's previous purchases but also on the purchases of other people who have bought similar books. As its customers' tastes and preferences evolve, Amazon's engagement with them reflects those changes. As the Internet takes hold in more fields, other companies will have to develop the interactive capabilities of an Amazon.com to keep customers engaged.

MOBILIZING CUSTOMER COMMUNITIES

A second reality that companies must face is that thanks to the Internet, customers in the new economy are finding it easier to form, on their own, self-selecting virtual communities. On-line customer communities can be quite tightly knit. Internet chat rooms, for example, are easy to start up, join, and participate in. Chat rooms accommodate a wide range of personalities—many of them assumed ones. Yet chat rooms aren't entirely unstructured. They often impose strict rules of dialogue and will expel individuals who break those rules.

The power of customer communities derives in large measure from the speed with which they can be mobilized.

Customer communities can exercise a powerful influence on the market. Take the Hollywood Stock Exchange, a simulated entertainment stock market in which "MovieStocks" and "StarBonds" are actively traded through a film's concept, development, production, wrap, and release. There are put and call options on opening-weekend losers and winners, and traders predict the four-week box office take for each film. The traders create news with their investment decisions, so major studios and actors cannot afford to ignore this customer community when shaping their development and marketing efforts.

The power of such communities derives in large measure from the speed with which they can be mobilized. Word spreads so fast on the Internet that people now refer to word of mouth as "viral marketing." That's already transforming the management of brands. In the past, companies pushed an image concept that was positioned through advertising, packaging, and so on, to individual consumers. But in the new market, positioning evolves with consumers' collective personalized experiences. Consider Netscape, Yahoo!, Amazon, eBay, E*Trade, and Excite. In each case, it was the customers who forged and legitimized the evolving identities of those companies and gave them meaning as brands in the new economy.

Smart companies are finding ways to mobilize customer communities. The Dutch giant Philips Electronics is a case in point. One of the company's customers recently set up a Web site for hackers who are interested in exploring embedded software for the Pronto, Philips's intelligent universal remote control. The site makes it easy to exchange program files, codes, and other information, and manufacturers of audio-video products post their software code to help people save programming time. The hackers, in exploring ways to make the product more user-friendly, benefit both the consumers and the company. Philips tapped into and mobilized a self-selected community created independently by consumers.

MANAGING CUSTOMER DIVERSITY

As companies embrace the market as a forum, they become more vulnerable to customer diversity. That is particularly true of companies that sell technology-intensive products, which are sensitive to variations in customers' sophistication.

Consumers' experiences of a technology product or service—and therefore their judgment of that product or service—will vary according to their skills as users.

For instance, it can take anywhere from five minutes to several hours for people to learn to use a new software application. This sophistication gap isn't new; younger users have always been quicker than older ones to adopt new products and services. But information technology has served to widen the gap considerably.

A user's sophistication also determines his tolerance of problems. A gifted software engineer may happily pay for the privilege of getting a beta version of some software. The experience—the fun and the pleasure—for this person is in finding the bugs. But others see software as a grim necessity—the last thing they want to experience is a system error.

Consumer concerns about privacy and security can also accentuate the diversity among users. Consider Microsoft's e-mail service, Hotmail, which reportedly has more than 30 million subscribers. Microsoft does not charge its subscribers for the Hotmail service, but it does require that subscribers provide information about themselves, which the company can use to solicit advertisers. Nearly all the "free" services available on the Internet are based on this model. But many consumers don't like to provide such information and would rather go without the service or pay a fee instead. Security on the Internet is also a hot issue with consumers. While some people will happily buy a car on-line, others are uncomfortable about e-mailing credit card information. Companies that ignore such differences among consumers do so at their own peril.

Apart from technology, globalization in the marketplace also heightens variation in customer sophistication. Consider the telecommunications industry. For instance, Lucent Technologies has to contend with battalions of new and unknown customers, many of whom have limited or no knowledge of the telecom business. The only

common denominator among them is a desire to participate in the telecommunications revolution. For managers
at Lucent, who are used to working with a handful of
large, highly skilled, established customers like AT&T and
the regional Bell operating companies, this proliferation
of unsophisticated customers poses unsettling questions.
How does one respond to a Thai investor who wants a
wireless system set up in six months? More and more
companies are facing this kind of dilemma.

COCREATING PERSONALIZED EXPERIENCES

Harnessing the competencies of the consumer involves
more than just setting up a dialogue. Managers also have
to realize that the customer is no longer interested in
buying a product. The product, in fact, is no more than
an artifact around which customers have experiences.
What's more, customers are not prepared to accept
experiences fabricated by companies. Increasingly, they
want to shape those experiences themselves, both indi-
vidually and with experts or other customers.

   It is important to distinguish personalization from
customization. Customization assumes that the manufacturer will design a product to suit a customer's needs.
It is particularly pronounced over the Web, where consumers can customize a host of products and services
such as business cards, computers, greeting cards, mort-
gages, and flowers simply by choosing from a menu of
features. Personalization, on the other hand, is about the
customer becoming a cocreator of the content of their
experiences. An on-line florist, for example, would let
customers specify and design the type, quantity, and
arrangement of flowers, vases, and colors they desired,
rather than forcing the customer to pick from a menu of
services. The florist would also make it possible for the

customer to discuss his or her ideas with in-house experts and other customers.

Companies in the entertainment and education businesses have gone perhaps the furthest in engaging the customer in the personalization of his experiences. Consider a visitor to the Whitney Museum in New York. Visitors previously had the option of taking a guided or an unguided tour. Today, they can tour the museum themselves with the help of a multimedia pad PC that blends audio, text, and video; they can tour the museum with human guides who have varying levels of expertise; or they can tour the museum with both multimedia and human guides. People can design their visit according to what they know and what they want to know.

Managing the Personalized Experience

To provide personalized experiences, companies must create opportunities for customers to experiment with and then decide the level of involvement they want in creating a given experience with a company. Since the level of customer engagement cannot be predetermined, companies will have to give consumers as much choice and flexibility as possible—in the channels of distribution and communication and in the design of products. But companies can also help direct their customers' expectations by guiding public debate about the future of technology and the economy.

MANAGING MULTIPLE CHANNELS OF EXPERIENCES

As the case of Amazon.com illustrates, the Web is an incredibly rich channel for direct dialogue. It has also spawned more efficient business models. Indeed, some people have argued that the virtual distribution channels provided by the Internet will completely displace traditional channels in some industries because of their cost advantages. A bank, for example, saves 80% of its costs when customers transact business using a PC; the customer also saves time and travel costs. But research shows that a consumer's experience with a company is highly influenced by the environment in which it occurs. Wells Fargo, for instance, tried to force its customers to use PC-based banking services, without much success. Customers became dissatisfied, and profits eroded. Thus, the method by which customers and companies communicate is an integral part of creating an experience. The more environments a company can provide, the richer its customers' experiences are likely to be.

For example, the Borders Books Web site and the layout of its bricks-and-mortar stores and cafés reinforce each other. Borders' customers like to browse among real books as well as virtual books, and they enjoy a good café latte while doing either. That's why Borders has computer terminals as well as books in its stores and cafés. And it's surely significant that about two-thirds of Charles Schwab's customers are still recruited through its bricks-and-mortar branches, where they can engage in personalized, educational discussions. In fact, the traditional distribution channels are likely to evolve. Take banks again. Although most customers are likely to migrate to ATMs, PCs, and cellular phones to transact their banking, there could still be a role for branch networks as private clubs for rich pensioners, especially in places like Florida, or simply as havens for the elderly.

It's likely, therefore, that most companies will find that they have to manage—and integrate—several distribution channels. A key challenge will be to ensure that the nature and quality of the fulfillment, the personalized experience for the individual, is not very different across the channels. One problem companies face is that their established channel partners are likely to resist this type of move: Why should car dealers want to let Ford or General Motors sell directly through the Internet? Other companies will find resistance from within. Pressure from their own brokers and agents delayed financial service companies such as Merrill Lynch and Aetna from offering on-line services. As a result, much of the progress in virtual distribution channels so far has been made by newcomers such as E*Trade and Priceline.com.

The biggest challenge for companies, however, will be to develop the infrastructures needed to support a multi-channel distribution network. For some businesses, especially those in traditional industries, the most pressing questions relate to their information technologies, which must evolve to cope with newer channels of communication and logistics. One of the most critical elements in the information infrastructure is a company's billing system, which is an invaluable repository of customer information. The problem is that many companies that now have to deal directly with consumers lack any competence in billing because they relied in the past on their channel partners to handle that task.

The challenges of building and integrating a virtual channel pale beside the challenges faced by the Internet companies themselves. It's no longer about e-commerce, but f-commerce—the fulfillment of goods and services that can't be downloaded. As one manager remarked: "Anyone can sell a book on the Internet; delivering it to the individual expeditiously and at a very low cost is the problem." The archetypal Internet company, Amazon.com soon is expected to have 3.5 million square feet of distribution space at seven centers nationwide—more than ten times the company's fulfillment capacity last year. And Webvan Group, a fast-growing on-line grocery merchant, placed a $1 billion order for the Bechtel group to build highly automated warehouses in 26 markets across the United States.

The realization that the product is subordinate to the experience will force managers to throw out their old assumptions about product development.

Achieving low-cost delivery in the new economy requires that companies combine their telecommunications and Internet infrastructure with a physical logistics and service infrastructure. Few Internet companies can manage physical delivery at all, let alone combine it with anything. Significantly, the companies that have developed the most effective integrated logistics systems are manufacturers. Toyota, for example, has announced that it can take an order on the Internet and deliver a customized car within a week. In the computer industry, the outstanding example is Dell, which offers built-to-order PCs directly over the Internet.

MANAGING VARIETY AND EVOLUTION

The realization that the product is subordinate to the experience will force managers to throw their old assumptions about product development out the window. Managers previously focused on understanding how to use technology to generate variety in products and on managing the way technology evolves. Technology road maps are a staple in most research and development groups. Concepts such as platforms, generations, models, versions, releases, upgrades, options, and bundles pervade the R&D departments of most high-technology companies. Indeed, all that mapping has enabled companies to create the customized products we now take for granted.

Unfortunately, customers find complicated menus very annoying and judge a company's products not by their features but by the degree to which a product or a service gives them the experiences they want. Consider a product that may incorporate, say, 20 functions. A user may need only five of those functions, and she does not want to go through the trouble of searching for her preferred features every time she uses the product. The driver of a luxury car equipped with a navigation system might want to use the system only to get a map and check the number of miles to his destination. However many capabilities the navigation system has, that driver will judge the system's performance according to the ease with which he can do those things. Why can't features used most often float to the top in interfaces? Why can't products reveal more sophisticated features and functionality as the user evolves?

The point is, managing the variety of customer experiences is not the same as managing variety in products. It is about managing the interface between a company and its customers; the range of experience transcends the company's products. Managers must develop a product that shapes itself to users' needs, not the other way around. But as noted, customers evolve over time through their experience with a product. The product has to evolve in a way that enables future modifications and extensions based both on customers' changing needs and on the company's changing capabilities.

But creating evolvable products and services isn't easy. The same customers who demand adaptability also expect 100% reliability. Computer manufacturers learned that the hard way when they tried to incorporate TV features into their PC-processor-powered products. The lesson? Consumers simply will not put up with a systems crash in the middle of their favorite sitcom. Companies in high-volume electronics still rely heavily on embedded processors, or microchips that contain built-in software programs designed to accomplish dedicated tasks. With embedded processors, companies can give products such as microwaves, automobiles, and VCRs the capacity to respond to an enormous variety of commands without breaking down. Indeed, the sales of embedded processors—even excluding those used in control applications for automobiles, microwave ovens, and can openers—are expected to be triple the number of PC-processor sales in the next five years.

But an embedded processor isn't the same as embedded intelligence. The products that have gone the furthest toward genuine embedded intelligence are in education and games. For example, children's educational software from the Learning Company adapts the level of difficulty and tasks based on the skills of the child using it. It recognizes the individual's accomplishment before presenting a new and more demanding task.

In consumer electronics, the product that has gone the furthest in this direction is TiVo, a home entertainment product from Philips. A little like Amazon.com, TiVo stores its user's viewing history and checks it against the programming of the channels it can access. The machine then recommends programs for the user and records them digitally as they are being broadcast. There's no need to preprogram a cantankerous VCR. The technology even lets viewers pause and replay during live broadcasts, which will be much appreciated by sports viewers the world over.

SHAPING CUSTOMERS' EXPECTATIONS

Harnessing customer competence and managing person-alized experiences requires cooperation from consumers. They must be sensitive to "what is next"—and that means companies must shape their expectations.

Many chief executives have tried to shape consumer expectations. Bill Gates, for example, has used his two books—*The Road Ahead* and *Business @ the Speed of Thought*—to lead consumers' expectations of technology in the future. But there are some dangers for the unwary CEO. In the classroom, for example, teachers who go too fast can lose the attention of their students. So it was with John Sculley, former CEO of Apple Computer, who championed the concept of personal digital assistants in general and the Apple Newton in particular. He posi-tioned the Newton as a mass-market product when, in fact, it was too early in its development for the Newton to be made generally available. Sculley lost his audience. Consumers had a low tolerance for glitches in a product that was meant to be used by "Joe, the common man," and not "Jane, the computer whiz," on an all-day, every-day basis. For Newton, a first-generation product, that was devastating.

Shaping expectations is not just about traditional one-way communication by managers or advertising. It is about engaging current and potential consumers in public debate. It is about educating customers and being educated. Companies that are trying to introduce radical new technologies have a particular interest in educating their consumers. Monsanto discovered this the hard way. Its failure to shape expectations of consumer groups— especially skeptical groups in Europe and in Asia—about the benefits and limitations of genetically modified seeds has left the company facing massive resistance not only to its products but even to the very concept of genetic modification on which the company has staked its future. Educated customers can be advocates and activists for the company. For instance, Amway, Avon, or Mary Kay customers don't just sell and buy products; they advocate a particular Avon or Amway lifestyle. Likewise, Macintosh and PalmPilot users are fervent customers and activists. The battle for shaping expectations of "what is next" will require active and evangelical support from customers.

Customers as Competitors

Although managers can regard the customer as a source of competence, they also have to face the reality that their customers are becoming their competitors. Customers can extract value in ways that were unimaginable even three years ago.

In the traditional marketplace, companies had far better access to information than individual consumers did. That allowed companies to set prices based on their costs or their perceptions of the value of their products and services to their customers. But thanks to the Internet, customers and companies now have much the same information available to them, and there has been a consequent shift in power.

Armed with knowledge, customers are much more willing to negotiate terms and prices with companies. It's perfectly feasible for a customer to approach a bank and say, "I will always leave a $5,000 balance in the bank. These are the services I want free in return for this commitment." In some cases, customers even assess their own lifetime value to a company and use the knowledge to bargain for better terms. A customer at one telecom provider, a heavy user of long-distance services, even obtained preferential long-distance rates in exchange for a commitment to that provider.

It's not just the way that consumers judge and negotiate the price for a product that's changing; it's the price-setting mechanism itself. The popularity of businesses such as eBay and Priceline.com suggests that the auction is increasingly serving as the basis for pricing goods and services on-line. From the customer's perspective, the advantage of the auction process is that prices truly reflect the *utility to that customer*, at a point in time, of the goods and services being purchased. That doesn't mean prices are lower, only that the customer pays according to her need rather than according to the company's need. Managers everywhere will have to get used to the idea that they are price takers as well as price makers.

Traditional pricing won't disappear entirely. But as customers become more knowledgeable and recognize that they have choices and the power to negotiate, more businesses—from automakers to cosmetic-surgery clinics—will feel pressure to adopt an implicit (if not an explicit) auction process.

Preparing the Organization

Readying the organization for customer competence in the new economy will require a major overhaul of the traditional governance systems and organizational structures of the company. For a start, accounting standards in the new economy need to factor in intellectual and human capital. The GAAP-based accounting systems that all companies use today were designed for stable business environments in which the most important assets were physical, such as inventory, land, and buildings. Investment in these assets is treated as a capital investment, while investment in intangible assets, such as training, is treated as an expense. But the competence of customers is an intangible asset, often a matter of knowledge and skill. It should be considered capital.

Engaging in dialogue with a diverse and evolving customer base in multiple channels will place a high premium on organizational flexibility.

Traditional market systems were designed to focus on allocating costs, which used to be the main determinant of price. But as auctions become a bigger factor in pricing, the importance of cost allocation declines. The systems are also ill equipped to cater to the constant reconfiguration of the supply chain that will result from the existence of multiple distribution channels. Increasingly, companies will have to adopt a project-management approach to evaluating the performance of people and businesses rather than rely on quarterly and annual budget reviews. In this way, managers will be able to judge the performance of individuals and teams over time while retaining the power to change the composition and tasks of the teams they lead.

The organizational consequences of competing in the market as a forum will, if anything, be even more drastic. Engaging in a dialogue with a diverse and evolving customer base in multiple channels will place a high premium on organizational flexibility. In fact, no part of the company—a single salesperson or an entire business unit—will be able to assume that its role in the organization is stable. As business models are revised and new challenges and opportunities emerge, the organization will constantly have to reconfigure its resources—its people, machines, infrastructure, and capital. Managers have to create Velcro organizations, in which resources can be reconfigured seamlessly and with as little effort as possible—as in Velcro hooking and unhooking.

But the creation of a flexible organization will impose psychological and emotional traumas on the organization's employees. There is a limit to an individual's elasticity. There is a reason why start-ups have fewer problems in pushing the frontier of established business practices than established firms do—it's easier to start something new than it is to change something old. Managers must be prepared to deal with these traumas even as they identify the business challenges they face. The new marketplace will place a premium on managers who have collaboration and negotiation training. Learning, teaching, and transferring knowledge across boundaries will become essential skills. So, too, will the ability to attract—and retain—the right employees. In an era when the pace of change keeps accelerating, the only way to stay ahead is to hire people who are self-motivated to change.

It may sound paradoxical, but rapid change requires that companies have a stable center. Although products, services, channels, and business models can change with impunity, human beings—especially those who are healthy enough to change—still require some emotional anchors. The real challenge for senior managers will be to provide that stability while embracing change. The only way to do that is to develop a strong set of organizational values. That's not an easy task. It is easier to pay lip service to values than it is to live by them. Consider diversity in the workplace. It is a value professed by nearly all consulting firms—whose employees remain depressingly similar in age, class, and educational background. Providing stability in the new economy demands leadership that is intellectually vigorous and, at the same time, administratively savvy. The ability to amplify weak signals, interpret their consequences, and reconfigure resources faster than competitors will be a source of advantage. It's not just "running faster" but "thinking faster and smarter" that matters.

The new frontier for managers is to create the future by harnessing competence in an enhanced network that includes customers. To be serious about the new economy, you're going to have to be the part you're playing. As Hamlet said, you "must have that within which passeth show."

Note

1. See Gary Hamel and C.K. Prahalad, "The Core Competence of the Corporation," *HBR* May–June 1990.

Originally published in January–February 2000
Reprint R00108

Get Inside the Lives of Your Customers

PATRICIA B. SEYBOLD

Executive Summary

MANY COMPANIES HAVE become adept at the art of customer relationship management. They've collected mountains of data on preferences and behavior, divided buyers into ever-finer segments, and refined their products, services, and marketing pitches.

But all too often those efforts are too narrow—they concentrate only on the points where the customer comes into contact with the company. Few businesses have bothered to look at what the author calls the *customer scenario*—the broad context in which customers select, buy, and use products and services. As a result, consultant Patricia Seybold maintains, they've routinely missed chances to deepen loyalty and expand sales.

In this article, the author shows how effective three very different companies have been at using customer scenarios as the centerpiece of their marketing plans.

Chip maker National Semiconductor looked beyond the purchasing agents that buy in bulk to find ways to make it easier for engineers to design National's components into their specifications for mobile telephones. Each time they do so, it translates into millions of dollars in orders.

By developing a customer scenario that describes how people actually shop for groceries, Tesco learned the importance of decentralizing its Web shopping site and how the extra costs of decentralization could be outweighed by the higher profit margins online customers generate. And Buzzsaw.com used customer scenarios as the basis for its entire business. It has used the Web to create a better way for the dozens of participants in a constructions project to share their drawings and manage their projects.

Seybold lays out the steps managers can take to develop their own customer scenarios. By thinking broadly about the challenges your customers face, she suggests, you can almost always find ways to make their lives easier—and thus earn their loyalty.

OVER THE LAST DECADE, many companies have become adept at the art of customer relationship management. They've collected and sifted mountains of data on preferences and behavior, divided buyers into ever-finer segments, and honed their products, services, and marketing pitches. But something's been missing from these efforts: the big picture. Few companies have bothered to look carefully at the broad context in which customers select, buy, and use products and services. They've been so focused on fine-tuning their own offerings that they've failed to see how those products and services fit into the real lives of their customers. As a result, companies have routinely missed chances to expand sales and deepen loyalty.

Here's a simple example. Two shoppers go into Best Buy looking for new refrigerators. To the salesclerk who waits on them, the customers seem identical. But their situations couldn't be more different. The first shopper needs a new refrigerator to replace one that died the night before. Her goal is to keep her ice cream frozen, not to spend a lot of time browsing. The second shopper is looking for a refrigerator for a new house he's having built. He's got plenty of time to compare features and prices before making a purchase.

When the salesclerk treats these two customers the same, Best Buy loses out on some big opportunities. The time-pressed first shopper, for instance, values delivery speed above all else. If the clerk could offer her expedited delivery—that afternoon, perhaps—she would likely buy a refrigerator immediately, even if the premium delivery service involved a hefty surcharge. The second shopper is not a likely candidate for a quick sale, but he's a great candidate for aggressive cross-selling and relationship building. After all, he's probably going to be in the market for many other appliances for his new house. Best Buy might even want to offer him a free consulting service that would give him a comprehensive, customized plan for all the appliances he needs, a tailored delivery schedule, and a modest discount for his bulk order. But if the company doesn't know the customer's situation, it can only provide one-size-fits-all service.

Thinking in terms of customer scenarios has always been useful, but the arrival of the Internet makes the technique more powerful than ever.

I call the broad context in which a customer does business the *customer scenario*. In the Best Buy example, the first shopper's scenario might be called "emergency replacement"; the second shopper's, "furnish a home." By building a detailed understanding of common customer scenarios, a company can often find creative ways to expand its reach into the lives of buyers, helping them save time, use products and services more effectively, and fulfill supplementary needs that may not involve the company's offerings at all. In delivering such benefits, the company becomes a vastly more important—and much more indispensable—supplier to its customers.

Thinking in terms of customer scenarios has always been useful, but the arrival of the Internet makes the technique more powerful than ever. Because the Internet can deliver customized information and applications at a relatively low cost, companies can easily help customers carry out broad sets of activities. In this article, I will show how three very different companies—the chip maker National Semiconductor, the grocery chain Tesco, and the on-line marketplace Buzzsaw.com—have used customer scenarios as the centerpiece of their marketing plans, guiding the way they deliver value and use the Internet to buttress and extend their customer relationships.

Using Scenarios to Strengthen Relationships

National Semiconductor is one of the world's leading suppliers of analog and digital microchips, which process sounds and images in mobile phones, DVD players, cable boxes, and other electronic devices. The company has worked hard to build deep relationships with two distinct

sets of customers: design engineers and corporate purchasing agents. The design engineers are a particularly
critical audience. Although they don't directly buy parts
in bulk, the choices they make at the beginning of the
product development process determine the components
their companies or their manufacturing partners ultimately purchase, often in multimillion-dollar quantities.

In 1994, Phil Gibson, National's vice president of Web
business, led the establishment of a Web site to provide
design engineers with information about the company's
product line. The site was a success, but Gibson immediately saw that its potential would be far greater if it could
be expanded to address a wider set of engineers' needs.
In the late 1990s, therefore, he launched an ambitious
effort to develop a deep understanding of the scenarios
in which design engineers work and to create on-line
tools to support them.

The project initially focused on the design of power
supplies. Design engineers work under considerable time
pressure, and, typically, the last part of a design they
need to finish is the power supply module. Gibson and
his team saw that by providing easy-to-use tools to speed
the design of power supplies, they could attract engineers to National's site and influence the choices they
made.

Gibson assembled a SWAT team to craft the power-
supply design scenario. Made up of specialists in marketing, applications, and Web design, the team met with a
variety of engineers and learned about the tasks required
to design a power supply. They boiled their findings
down to a simple, four-step scenario:

1. Choose a part.

2. Create a design.

3. Analyze the design (using powerful simulation tools).

4. Build a prototype.

The team then created a set of on-line applications, which they dubbed Webench, that would give engineers all the tools they needed to carry out this scenario. Customers could complete the entire design process on National's site without having to run special software or buy expensive systems.

Here's how it works: an engineer logs on to Webench and is prompted to specify the overall parameters for the power supply and to identify the key components needed. The system automatically generates possible designs, along with complete technical specifications, parts lists, prices, and cost-benefit analyses. The engineer then refines the designs until one appears to satisfy the requirements. He or she can then run real-time simulations of the design, using a sophisticated software application National has licensed and offers on its site. The engineer can alter the design and simulate it as many times as necessary and then save all the iterations in a private portfolio—or even e-mail links to colleagues so they can run the saved simulations.

Once the engineer settles on a final design to be tested, the system can generate a bill of materials for creating a prototype. The parts list includes not only National's components but all the required components from other manufacturers as well. It even has links to distributors that carry those parts, listing their current prices. And because National's site is tied in directly to the distributors' inventory systems, the engineer can order the parts with a single click.

When Gibson's team rolled out Webench in 1999, it decided to charge engineers for using the simulation tool to recoup the costs of licensing the software. But while engineers came to the Web site in droves, most backed out when they were asked for a credit card number. So Gibson switched gears and made the simulation tool available for free. Instead of nickel-and-diming the customers, he saw that the company could reap bigger rewards down the line: large orders for National's parts.

The strategy worked. Design engineers loved Webench, using it to design more than 20,000 power supplies in its first year of operation. Customers have found they can accomplish in a few hours what it previously took them months to do. And they now have the time to explore alternatives—time they would never have taken before. One engineer went through more than 250 design iterations for a single project; most go through five to ten. As Martin Volk, a customer from Motorola's Cellular Systems division, says: "Using these tools, I can go from an idea to a working prototype in a few clicks. National has thought of everything I need— from a huge catalog of parts to fast simulations."

The enthusiastic reaction spurred Gibson and his team to explore more customer scenarios. They asked engineers about other activities they were having trouble completing efficiently. In response, engineers said they wanted to subject complete product designs to thermal simulations; few of them had access to the sophisticated systems needed for such tests. The company created WebTherm, licensing state-of-the-art thermal simulation software and providing it for free to engineers to use on National's site. Other engineers asked the company to help them design more of the circuitry, not just the power supplies, for mobile phones on-line. This request resulted in a new set of scenarios for engineers who design wireless devices. (See the exhibit "National Semiconductor's Customer Scenario.")

By the fall of 2000, when National rolled out its WebTherm and Wireless design tools, 31,000 individuals were visiting the company's Web site and generating 3,000 orders or referrals to distributors every day. Most were orders for a small number of sample parts for prototyping, but the company expects each early design win to translate into millions of dollars in sales. As Gibson

National Semiconductor's Customer Scenario

National Semiconductor offers a sophisticated set of Web tools to help engineers design mobile phones and other electronic devices. This chart shows the steps an engineer would go through to design the power supply and circuitry for a mobile phone using National's on-line system.

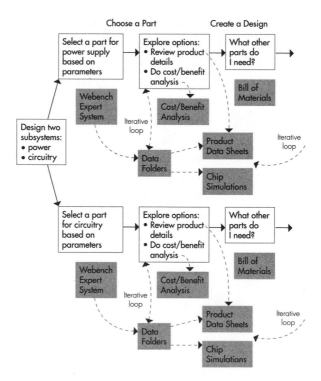

points out, "One integrated-socket win with Nokia translates into 40 million units for us."

In the year and a half that the company has been offering its scenario-based tools, National says, it knows that it has saved its customers an average of 50 hours per design, representing an average savings of $3,000. That amounts to a total customer savings of more than $135

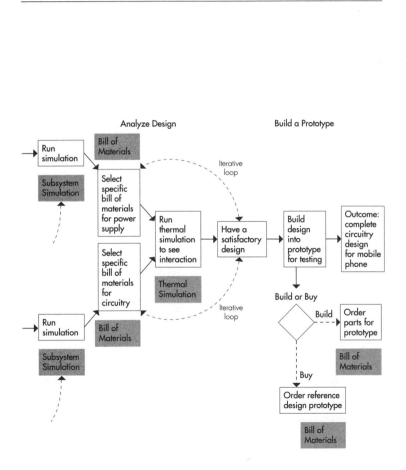

million so far on labor alone. With that kind of payback, the engineers have a strong incentive to continue using National's sites—and that seems to be exactly what they're doing.

National benefits in another important way, as well. By carefully monitoring the number and type of designs customers complete, the company is better able to predict the number and type of parts it will need to manufacture. These "buying signals," as the company calls them, enhance National's own operating efficiency.

Using Customer Scenarios to Guide Web Strategy

Despite much initial hype, most Internet grocery stores have struggled to attract customers and make money. But there's one shining exception: Tesco. A UK-based supermarket chain with annual revenues of £19 billion, the company launched Tesco Direct, its on-line sales channel, in late 1996, and today it is the world's largest and most profitable Internet grocer. Much of its success can be traced to the insights the company gained by thinking carefully about the typical grocery shopper's customer scenario and how that scenario could best be supported through a combination of stores and direct Internet sales.

Tesco quickly rejected one of the basic tenets underlying the strategies of most on-line grocers: consolidating inventory and fulfillment operations in a central warehouse to reduce costs.

The traditional customer scenario for grocery shopping has six steps:

1. Decide what my family needs this week.

2. Make a shopping list.

3. Go to the store.

4. Select groceries and pay for them.

5. Take them home.

6. Put them away.

Tesco thought that on-line sales could save customers considerable time and effort in steps 2 through 5. Customers could automate the creation of their grocery lists based on their prior purchases and avoid having to drive to and from stores, lugging heavy bags around. But when the company talked to its customers and watched their behavior, it found that the vast majority of them enjoyed shopping in stores—they liked to examine and touch the fresh produce and see what new products had been stocked on the shelves. They also trusted their local supermarkets, counting on them to provide quality goods at fair prices. Most customers did not see on-line shopping as a substitute for traditional shopping; they saw it as a complement, a way to save time when they were in a hurry.

Based on this understanding of customers' preferences, Tesco set out to tightly integrate its off-line and on-line offerings so that customers could streamline their shopping scenarios without sacrificing flexibility. Gary Sargeant, a former store manager who now heads up Tesco Direct, quickly rejected one of the basic tenets underlying the strategies of most on-line grocers: consolidating inventory and fulfillment operations in a central warehouse to reduce costs. He knew that customers would prefer to purchase on-line from the store in which they normally shopped in person. That way, they would always be charged the same prices and have the same selection of products no matter how they decided to buy; there would be no discord between the two scenarios.

To carry out its plan, Tesco Direct had to link its on-line shopping application directly to each store's pricing and inventory systems. That benefited both the customer and the company. It significantly raised the odds that all the products a customer ordered would be available. And because the servers in each store could save a history of each customer's favorite products—both those ordered on-line and those scanned through the checkout in the markets—the stores could fine-tune their wholesale orders to ensure that key products were always on hand. The "shop on-line from my store" scenario also allowed the company to maintain regional variations in pricing, boosting its overall profits.

Of course, the decentralized strategy raised operational challenges. To meet them, Sargeant handpicked a team of logisticians to help design the optimal in-store pick-and-pack system to fill the on-line orders. It works like this: order pickers in the stores use shopping carts specially equipped with six trays and an on-line display. The display shows the pickers their routes through the store—each route is designed to avoid peak traffic areas (to go to the fresh fish counter at, say, 4 PM or the produce section at 6 PM)—and lists the items to be picked as they go down each aisle. Items are scanned as they're dropped into each customer's tray, so they can't be mixed up. And if an item has gone out of stock in the few hours that elapsed since the order was placed, the picking application proposes an alternate product from a list of items that the customer previously purchased.

Once the shopping cart is filled, the trays are loaded directly into delivery vans that wait behind each store. Deliveries are scheduled according to customers' preferences (within a two-hour delivery window to allow for traffic delays), and the vans' routes are optimized to ensure that produce and other perishable goods are delivered fresh. Any items that have been substituted are carefully placed on top so they can be reviewed and accepted or rejected when the order is delivered.

Tesco Direct takes the customer's experience very seriously. It rigorously monitors on-time deliveries, order accuracy, and customer satisfaction. It also simulates its customers' on-line experience by running shopping-scenario robots using a variety of different browsers, Internet service providers, and dial-in numbers. It uses "sanity checks" as well. By trial and error, for instance, the company discovered that if any store's orders fall 15% below the volume for the same time period on the previous day, there may be a technical problem. A simple alert goes off whenever such a drop occurs.

Tesco's Web operation has been a great success. By September 2000, Tesco.com had 750,000 registered customers and extended its reach to cover 90% of the United Kingdom. The site had processed more than a million orders, delivering each week an average of 60,000 orders, which generate revenues of more than £5 million. And, as Tesco foresaw, the site has not displaced its traditional stores. Fully 75% of on-line shoppers also shop in their local market.

What about profits? Obviously, it costs more for Tesco to fill an on-line order than to let customers do the shopping themselves. In recognition of that fact, the company charges customers £5 per delivery, a fee that covers 60% of the added operational costs. The remaining costs are covered by the on-line shoppers themselves, who tend to order more profitable items than in-store shoppers. According to Sargeant, the mix of products Tesco's Internet shoppers order is two to three percentage points more profitable than that of the average in-store order. At least some of the added profit results from the Web site's ability to cross-sell and up-sell. When a customer checks off an item (such as bread), other related items (such as marmalade or butter) pop up on the screen. The total profit margin for Tesco's on-line shoppers, after all operational costs, runs between 10% and 12%.

Using Customer Scenarios as Business Models

Scenario thinking can help companies dramatically improve customers' experiences and strengthen their loyalty. But there's also another big potential benefit. In many cases, a close examination of customer scenarios can spur innovative ideas for entirely new businesses. That's exactly how Autodesk, which with roughly 80% of the market is the world's leading provider of PC computer-aided design software, came to create its successful spin-off Buzzsaw.com.

In late 1996, Anne Bonaparte, a member of Autodesk's sales organization, asked customers in the construction business how they used the company's applications in designing buildings and what they wanted in future releases. She got a surprising answer. "Don't give us more CAD functionality," customers said. "We need help getting these construction projects completed. There are too many places where things slip through the cracks." One customer told her about a problem he had in designing a chip-manufacturing facility for Intel. He had sent some architectural drawings as e-mail attachments, but they didn't make it through the company's Internet fire wall, and an entire day was lost on the project. "When you lose a day in building an Intel fabrication plant, you're losing $1 million!" he exclaimed.

That story and others got Bonaparte to thinking: why not create a better way for the dozens of participants in a construction project to share their drawings electronically and manage their projects from end to end? Thanks to computerized design tools and the Internet, engineers, architects, contractors, and building owners were doing most of their collaborating electronically, but there was no efficient and dependable way for them to manage all the complex interactions or to exchange widely divergent types of computer files. Bonaparte came to believe that a well-designed Internet work space could find great success in the market. From that idea, Buzzsaw.com was born.

The team that launched Buzzsaw.com conducted extensive research into the ways the various participants in construction projects worked. They recruited an advisory board of six professionals to ensure that customers' points of view guided every decision they made. From the research, the team laid out a high-level customer scenario for construction projects:

1. Set project scope, schedule, and budget.

2. Gain financial backing.

3. Recruit the team.

4. Develop the design.

5. Produce the plans and specifications.

6. Manage the bidding and negotiations.

7. Manage the construction process.

8. Manage the facility

The team recognized, however, that this scenario was just a broad framework; there were many variations. A renovation project, for instance, often skipped the first two steps. Moreover, all the participants, from architects to bankers to plumbers, had their own scenarios, which played out within the larger one. And they all tended to work in idiosyncratic ways, following different processes, using different software, and even defining projects very differently. The team saw that the secret to success lay not in imposing rigid scenarios on customers but in providing on-line tools that would allow customers to design their own scenarios.

In conceiving its on-line work space, Buzzsaw.com initially focused on the central step in the general scenario: developing the design. It created a site in which building owners, architects, engineers, and other construction professionals could work together through the highly iterative process of reaching consensus on a building's design. The site allows participants to store and access building plans, schedules, contracts, and procurement documents in all the common file formats. Team discussions, management decisions, and document revisions are automatically tracked. And team members collaborate to revise drawings in real time using on-line meeting tools. Most important, Buzzsaw.com provides a flexible work flow system that lets customers define rules for routing documents and messages among team members. Thus, the site can accommodate an infinite variety of customer scenarios.

From that starting point, Buzzsaw.com expanded the site to support other steps in the overall scenario.

Upstream, for example, the site includes a directory of local contractors and specialists to aid in recruiting a team, and it offers loan-processing and project-tracking tools for banks and other financial backers to use. Downstream, Buzzsaw.com offers tools to manage the production of specifications for the complex array of supplies involved in a typical project, as well as direct links to the reprographers that produce the actual blueprints and bid packages. It helps manage the bidding process by automatically distributing the bid packages and subsequent modifications to contractors and subcontractors. The site also lets subcontractors automatically solicit bids for materials from their own suppliers, thus streamlining the procurement process, which is essential to effective project management. (See the exhibit "Buzzsaw.com's Customer Scenario.")

Buzzsaw.com's model is very different from the popularly held notion of an electronic marketplace as an electronic catalog or auction. Very little buying or selling takes place. Rather, the site provides a framework for managing customers' end-to-end scenarios and offers access to the resources, services, and products required to fulfill those scenarios. Instead of making its money by exacting tiny commissions on transactions, Buzzsaw.com charges users subscription fees based on the amount of disk storage they use on the company's servers. It also earns supplementary revenues from licensing its Project Point software to reprographers and from fees for procurement and printing services.

After piloting the site with a core group of customers in late 1999, Buzzsaw.com began its marketing push in earnest in the first quarter of 2000. By then, it had already attracted about 230 customers, many of whom were running multiple projects on the site. Its clients

Buzzsaw.com's Customer Scenario

Recognizing that construction projects are highly collaborative, involving many different participants, Buzzsaw.com built its site to accommodate complex interactions. This chart shows the key steps in Buzzsaw.com's construction scenario and the range of participants involved.

Set Project Scope, Schedule, and Budget	Gain Financial Backing	Recruit the Team	Develop the Design	Produce the Plans and Specifications	Manage the Bidding and Negotiations	Manage the Construction Process	Manage the Facility

• **Project Owner**
• **Architect**
• **Engineers**
  – **Structural**
  – **Environmental**
• **Town Boards**
  – Zoning
  – Commerce
  – Urban Planning
	• **Owner**
	• **Architect**
	• Bank Loan Officer
	• Insurer
		• **Owner**
		• **Architect**
		• **Engineers**
		• **Contractors**
		• Loan Officer
			• **Owner**
			• **Architect**
			• **Engineers**
			• Loan Officer
			• Other Stakeholders
			  – Tenants
			  – Local Government
				• **Architect**
				• **Engineers**
				• **Owner**
				• **General Contractor**
				• Reprographers
					• **General Contractor**
					• **Engineers**
					• **Architect**
					• Subcontractors
					  – Electrician
					  – Plumber
					• Reprographers
						• **Construction Manager (represents owner)**
						• **General Contractor**
						• Subcontractors
						• Suppliers and Distributors
						• **Architects**
						• **Engineers**
						• Reprographers
							• **Owner**
							• Facility Manager

included large corporations such as DuPont and Walt
Disney; leading architecture and engineering firms such
as Ellerbe Becket and Skidmore, Owings & Merrill; and
many small architecture
firms. By November 2000, a
year after Buzzsaw.com
was officially launched,
20,000 projects were under
way. At an average of 7.5
users per project, that
works out to some 150,000
active users. Fifteen per-
cent of the customers were located outside the United
States, and several U.S.-based customers were using
Buzzsaw.com to manage projects remotely in countries
all around the world.

As I've watched companies struggle to streamline their customer-facing business processes, I've found that they don't know how to put themselves in their customers' shoes.

The most important factor driving Buzzsaw.com's
burgeoning success is the way its customers recruit more
customers. Typically, a new client, such as an architectural firm, will try out Buzzsaw.com through a pilot
project involving just a couple of people. For its next project, it will use Buzzsaw.com with its own clients and
partners. Those team members, in turn, will begin using
Buzzsaw.com for other projects. This is a true example of
viral marketing, and it happens because Buzzsaw.com
organized its site—indeed its entire business—around
the highly collaborative nature of the construction
scenario.

Getting Started with Scenarios

As I've watched companies struggle to streamline their
customer-facing business processes, I've found that they
don't know how to put themselves in their customers'

shoes. They may think they're taking the customer's perspective, but they're really only focused on the point at which the customer comes into contact with their company. That touch point is certainly important, but it's rarely the center of the customer's experience. It's just a way station on the road toward a broader goal.

Creating customer scenarios isn't particularly difficult, but it does require people to think beyond their companies' own processes and objectives. The best way to get started is to sit down and try to map out some simple scenarios. The first few will take some time, but once you get the hang of it, you'll be able to go much faster. Here are the basic steps:

- Select a target customer set. Be as explicit as possible (business travelers who use corporate travel agents, for example, or builders of housing developments).

- Select a goal that the customer needs to fulfill (changing travel itineraries in the middle of a trip, for instance, or providing home buyers with a customizable bill of materials for plumbing fixtures, lighting fixtures, carpeting, or appliances).

- Envision a particular situation for the customer (an exhausted traveler staying in a hotel overnight, say, or a contractor desiring one-stop pickup of supplies).

- Determine a start and an end point for the scenario. The end point is what the customer considers to be the successful achievement of his or her goals.

- Map out as many variations of each scenario as you can think of. Mentally walk through each step as if you were the customer.

- Think of the individual activities the customer performs and the information needed at every step. What can your company do to support those activities and supply that information? Where can you save the customer time and trouble? How might your involvement influence the buying choices the customer makes?

- How can you use your marketing, distribution, and service channels—your sales force, Web site, call center, and so on—to support and streamline the customer scenario? What new resources would you need? What process changes would you have to make? What technologies would you need to install?

You should go through this exercise for a number of different target customers, customer goals, and customer situations. By developing multiple scenarios, you'll begin to see patterns. Different scenarios may have critical steps in common; by focusing your initial efforts on these common steps, you'll get the most bang for your buck.

Once you have a sense of how customer scenarios work and what needs to be done to document them, it's time to call in the customers. You must test your assumptions with the real people who use your products and services, working with them to refine scenarios and produce new ones. Ultimately, the goal should be to empower your customers to define their scenarios for you. Sometimes, this can be accomplished with technology, by providing online tools for customizing work flows and activities, as Buzzsaw.com is doing. Other times, it means keeping the lines of communication wide open, as National Semiconductor strives to do. Finally, you'll want to closely monitor each customer scenario in as near to real time as possible. Tracking the way customers perform the steps that matter most to them can reveal further opportunities to enhance their overall experience.

We live in a time when customers are under unceasing pressure to do things more quickly, to cram more into each day. By thinking broadly about the challenges your customers face, rather than narrowly about what you can sell them, you can almost always find ways to make their lives easier. That, more than anything else, will earn you their loyalty.

Originally published in May 2001
Reprint R01015E

The Old Pillars of
New Retailing

LEONARD L. BERRY

Executive Summary

DESPITE THE HARSH REALITIES of retailing, the illusion persists that magical tools can help companies overcome the problems of fickle consumers, price-slashing competitors, and mood swings in the economy. Such wishful thinking holds that retailers will thrive if only they communicate better with customers through e-mail, employ hidden cameras to learn how customers make purchase decisions, and analyze scanner data to tailor special offers and manage inventory. But the truth is, there are no quick fixes.

In the course of his extensive research on dozens of retailers, Leonard Berry found that the best companies create value for their customers in five interlocking ways. Whether you're running a physical store, a catalog business, an e-commerce site, or a combination of the three, you have to offer your customers superior solutions to their needs, treat them with respect, and connect with them on an emotional level. You also have to set prices fairly and make it easy for people to find what they need, pay for it quickly, and then move on. None of these pillars is new, and each sounds exceedingly simple, but don't be fooled—implementing these axioms in the real world is surprisingly difficult.

The author illustrates how some retailers have built successful operations by attending to these common-sense ways of dealing with their customers and how others have failed to do so.

Everyone who glances at a newspaper knows that the retailing world is brutally competitive. The demise of Montgomery Ward in the realm of bricks and mortar as well as the struggles of eToys on-line—to choose only two recent examples—make it clear that no retailer can afford to be complacent because of previous successes or rosy predictions about the future of commerce.

Despite the harsh realities of retailing, the illusion persists that magical tools, like Harry Potter's wand, can help companies overcome the problems of fickle consumers, price-slashing competitors, and mood swings in the economy. The wishful thinking holds that retailers will thrive if only they communicate better with customers through e-mail, employ hidden cameras to learn how customers make purchase decisions, and analyze scanner data to tailor special offers and manage inventory.

But the truth of the matter is, there are no quick fixes. Yes, technology can help any business operate more effectively, but many new advances are still poorly understood—and in any case, retailing can't be reduced to tools and techniques. Over the past eight years, I've analyzed dozens of retail companies to understand the underlying differences between outstanding and mediocre performers. My research includes interviews with senior and middle managers and frontline employees, observations of store operations, and extensive reviews of published and internal company materials. I've found that the best retailers create value for their customers in five interlocking ways. Doing a good job in just three or four of the ways won't cut it; competitors will rush to exploit weakness in any of the five areas. If one of the pillars of a successful retailing operation is missing, the whole edifice is weakened. (See "Are Your Retailing Pillars Solid—or Crumbling?")

Today's shoppers want the total customer experience: superior solutions to their needs, respect, an emotional connection, fair prices, and convenience. Offering four out of the five pillars isn't enough; a retailer must offer all of them.

The key is focusing on the total customer experience. Whether you're running physical stores, a catalog business, an e-commerce site, or a combination of the three, you have to offer customers superior solutions to their needs, treat them with real respect, and connect with them on an emotional level. You also have to set prices fairly and make it easy for people to find what they need, pay for it, and move on. These pillars sound simple on paper, but they are difficult to implement in the real world. Taking each one in turn, we'll see how some retailers have built successful operations by attending to these commonsense ways of dealing with customers, and how others have failed to pay them the attention they require.

Pillar 1: Solve Your Customers' Problems

It has become commonplace for companies to talk about selling solutions rather than products or services. But what does this really mean for retailers? Put simply, it means that customers usually shop for a reason: they

---

Are Your Retailing Pillars Solid—or Crumbling?

	Inferior Retailers . . .	Superior Retailers . . .
Solutions	gather products, stack them on shelves, put price tags on them, and wonder where their customers are.	consider what people really need and how they can meet that particular need better than competitors can.
Respect	are staffed by people who don't know what customers want and aren't about to interrupt their conversations to find out.	actually train and manage the salespeople they hire so that they are courteous, energetic, and helpful to customers.
Emotions	act as if their customers are Spock-like Vulcans who make purchases solely according to cold logic.	recognize that everything about a retail experience sends a message to customers that goes to the heart, not just the brain.
Pricing	focus exclusively on their supposed low prices, often because they have nothing else of value to offer customers.	focus on having fair prices instead of playing mind games with "special offers," fine print, and bogus sales.
Convenience	are open for business when it's convenient for them, close checkout lanes when it's convenient for them, deliver products when it's convenient for them, and so on.	understand that people's most precious commodity in the modern world is time and do everything they can to save as much of it as possible for their customers.

have a problem—a need—and the retailer hopes to provide the solution. It's not enough, for example, just to sell high-quality apparel—many retailers do that. Focusing on solutions means employing salespeople who know how to help customers find clothing that fits and flatters, having tailors on staff and at the ready, offering home delivery, and happily placing special orders. Every retailer hopes to meet its customers' pressing needs; some do it much better than others.

The Container Store provides its customers with superior solutions. The 22-store chain, based in Dallas, averages double-digit annual sales growth by selling something that absolutely everyone needs: storage and organization products. From boxes and trunks to hangers, trays, and shelving systems, each store carries up to 12,000 different products.

The Container Store's core strategy is the same today as it was in 1978, when the company was founded: to improve customers' lives by giving them more time and space. The company accomplishes this mission well. It starts with the selection of merchandise, which must meet criteria for visibility, accessibility, and versatility. The company's philosophy is that its products should allow people to see what they've stored and get at it easily. The merchandise must also be versatile enough to accommodate customers' particular requirements.

Store organization is another key ingredient of superior solutions at the Container Store. The merchandise is organized in sections such as kitchen, closet, laundry, office, and so on. Many products are displayed in several sections because they can solve a variety of problems. A sweater box, for example, can also store office supplies. Plastic trash cans can also be used for dog food and recyclables. Individual products are often combined and sold as a system—thus, parents in the store who want to equip their children for summer camp may find a trunk filled with a laundry bag, a toothbrush case, a first-aid pouch, leakproof bottles, a "critter catcher," and other items.

Great service is another component of the Container Store's ability to solve its customers' storage problems. The company is very careful about hiring; it patiently waits until it finds just the right person for a position. Container Store employees are well trained to demonstrate how products work and to propose solutions to complex home organizational problems. They are also treated very well, both in terms of pay and in less tangible ways. In fact, the Container Store was ranked the best place to work in the country in 1999 and 2000 by *Fortune* magazine.

A relentless focus on solutions may sound simple, but it's not. The Container Store has many imitators, but none have matched it. Many businesses have only the fuzziest concept of selling solutions. Department store chains, for example, have stumbled in recent years. They lost their one-stop shopping advantage by eliminating many merchandise categories outside of apparel and housewares. And even as they focused on apparel, they lost ground both to specialty retailers that have larger category selections and to discounters that have lower prices. Finally, they lost their customer service advantage by employing salespeople who often are little more than poorly trained order takers. As a result, these stores do a relatively poor job of solving customers' problems. That's probably why only 72% of consumers shopped in department stores in 2000 compared with 85% in 1996.

Clearly, the lesson here is that you must understand what people need and how you're going to fill that need better than your competitors. The Container Store has figured this out; many department stores and other struggling retailers must go back to the beginning and answer these basic questions.

Pillar 2: Treat Customers with R-e-s-p-e-c-t

The best retailers show their customers what Aretha Franklin sang about: respect. Again, this is absolutely basic, and most retail executives would say that of course they treat customers with respect. But it just isn't so.

Everyone has stories to tell about disrespectful retailing. You're in an electronics store, looking for assistance to buy a DVD player or a laptop computer. You spot a couple of employees by their uniforms and badges, but they're deep in conversation. They glance in your direction but continue to ignore you. After awhile, you walk out, never to return.

Or you're in a discount store, looking for planters that have been advertised at a low price. You go to the store's garden center but cannot find the planters. This time, you succeed in flagging down an employee. You ask about the planters, but she just mumbles "I dunno" and walks away. Frustrated, you go to the customer service desk and ask the clerk where you might find the advertised planters. He suggests that you try the garden center. Once again, you head for the exit.

Disrespectful retailing isn't just about bored, rude, and unmotivated service workers. Cluttered, poorly organized stores, lack of signage, and confusing prices all show lack of respect for customers.

It's easy to go on. Stories about women trying to buy cars, as everyone knows, are enough to make your hair curl. The fact is, disrespectful retailing is pervasive. In the 2000 Yankelovich Monitor study of 2,500 consumers, 68% of those surveyed agreed with the statement that "Most of the time, the service people that I deal with for the products and services that I buy don't care much about me or my needs."

Disrespectful retailing isn't just about bored, rude, and unmotivated service workers. Cluttered, poorly organized stores, lack of signage, and confusing prices all show lack of respect for customers.

The best retailers translate the basic concept of respect into a set of practices built around people, policies, and place:

- They select, prepare, and manage their people to exhibit competence, courtesy, and energy when dealing with customers.

- They institute policies that emphasize fair treatment of customers—regardless of their age, gender, race, appearance, or size of purchase or account. Likewise, their prices, returns policy, and advertising are transparent.

- They create a physical space, both inside and outside the store, that is carefully designed to value customers' time.

In 1971, a 30-year-old entrepreneur named Len Riggio bought a floundering Manhattan bookshop called Barnes & Noble. Today, Barnes & Noble is the nation's largest bookseller, with fiscal 1999 sales of $3.3 billion. Respect for the customer has been at the heart of the company's rise.

Riggio's biggest idea was that books appeal to most everyone, not just to intellectuals, writers, and students in cosmopolitan cities. Riggio listened to prospective customers who wanted bigger selections of books, more convenient locations, and less intimidating environments. He put superstores in all types of communities, from big cities like Atlanta and Chicago, to smaller cities like Midland, Texas, and Reno, Nevada. His respect for the customer led him to create stores with spacious and comfortable interiors, easy chairs for relaxing with a book, and Starbucks coffee bars. To this day, he considers his best decision the installation of easy-to-find public restrooms in the stores. As he said in a recent speech, "You work so hard and invest so much to get people to visit your store, why would you want them to have to leave?"

Besides the large selection of books, the stores also have an active calendar of author signings, poetry readings, children's events, and book discussion groups. Many Barnes & Noble superstores have become a social arena in which busy consumers—who normally rush in and out of other stores—linger.

Riggio sees the Internet as much more than a way to deliver books to customers; it's another opportunity to listen to them and thus show respect for them. He views the store network and Barnesandnoble.com as portals to each other. Customers can ask salespeople at Internet service counters to search Barnesandnoble.com for out-of-stock books, for customer reviews of titles that interest them, and for information about authors, such as other books they've published. Customers in a superstore can order the books they want on-line and have them shipped either to that store or to any other address. If a return is necessary, customers can bring their on-line purchase back to the store.

The value of respect often gets little more than lip service from retailers. Some companies wait until it's too late to put words into action.

Pillar 3: Connect with Your Customers' Emotions

Most retailers understand in principle that they need to connect emotionally with consumers; a good many don't know how to (or don't try to) put the principle into practice. Instead, they neglect the opportunity to make emotional connections and put too much emphasis on prices. The promise of low prices may appeal to customers' sense of reason, but it does not speak to their passions.

Many U.S. furniture retailers are guilty of ignoring consumers' emotions. Although the average size of new homes in the country has grown by 25% since 1980, furniture accounts for a lower percentage of total U.S. consumer spending today (1%) than it did in 1980 (1.2%). Making consumers wait up to two months to receive their furniture contributes to these poor results. How can consumers get emotionally involved in products they know they won't see for weeks?

Poor marketing also hurts the industry. Most furniture stores focus strictly on price appeals, emphasizing cost savings rather than the emotional lift that can come from a new look in the home. "We don't talk about how easy it can be to make your home more attractive," says Jerry Epperson, an investment banker who specializes in the furniture industry. "All we talk about is 'sale, sale, sale' and credit terms."

Great retailers reach beyond the model of the rational consumer and strive to establish feelings of closeness, affection, and trust. The opportunity to establish such feelings is open to any retailer, regardless of the type of business or the merchandise being sold. Everyone is emotionally connected to some retailers—from local businesses such as the wine merchant who always remembers what you like; to national companies like Harley-Davidson, which connects people through its Harley Owners Group; to catalog retailer Coldwater Creek, which ships a substitute item to customers who need to make returns before the original item is sent back.

One retailer that has connected especially well with its target market in recent years is Journeys, a Nashville, Tennessee-based chain of shoe stores located primarily in shopping malls. The chain focuses on selling footwear to young men and women between the ages of 15 and 25. Started in 1987, Journeys didn't take off until 1995 when new management took over. The chain has achieved double-digit comparable-store sales increases in five of the six years since then and is now expanding by as many as 100 new stores per year.

Journeys has penetrated the skepticism and fickleness that are characteristic of many teens. By keeping a finger on the pulse of its target market, the company consistently has the right brands available for this especially brand-conscious group of consumers. Equally important, it creates the right store atmosphere—the stores pulsate with music, video, color, and brand merchandising.

A Journeys store is both welcoming and authentic to young people; it is simultaneously energetic and laid-back. Journeys' employees are typically young—the average age of a store manager is about 25—and they dress as they please. Customers frequently visit a store in groups just to hang out; salespeople exert no pressure to buy.

And everyone, whether they've made a purchase or not, usually leaves with a giveaway—for instance, a key chain, a compact-disc case, a promotional T-shirt, or one of the 10 million or so stickers the stores give out over the course of a year. The stickers, which usually feature one of the brands Journeys sells, often end up on backpacks, skateboards, school lockers, or bathroom mirrors. Journeys also publishes a bimonthly magazine, *Dig*, that is available in the stores, and it runs a Web site that seeks to replicate the atmosphere of its stores. The number of site visits explodes whenever the company's commercials appear on MTV.

Journeys works in large part because it has created an atmosphere that connects emotionally with the young people it serves. Other retailers should bear in mind that it takes more than a room full of products with price tags on them to draw people in.

Pillar 4: Set the Fairest (Not the Lowest) Prices

Prices are about more than the actual dollars involved. If customers suspect that the retailer isn't playing fair, prices can also carry a psychological cost. Potential buyers will not feel comfortable making purchases if they fear that prices might be 30% lower next week, or if certain charges have only been estimated, or if they are unsure whether an advertised sale price represents a genuine markdown.

Consider some of the pricing tactics commonly used by certain home improvement retailers. One well-known company advertises products as "special buys" even though it has not lowered the regular prices. Another purposely misrepresents a competitor's prices on price-comparison signs within its stores. Still another company promotes lower-grade merchandise implying that it is top quality. One retailer puts a disclaimer in its ads that reads: "Prices in this ad may be different from the actual price at time of purchase. We adjust our prices daily to the lumber commodity market." The disclaimer paves the way for the retailer to raise its prices regardless of the advertised price.

Excellent retailers seek to minimize or eliminate the psychological costs associated with manipulative pricing. Most of these retailers follow the principles of "everyday fair pricing" instead of "everyday low pricing." A fact of retail life is that no retailer, not even Wal-Mart, can truthfully promise customers that it will always have the lowest prices. An uncomfortable truth for many retailers is that their "lowest price anywhere" positioning is a crutch for the lack of value-adding innovation. Price is the only reason they give customers to care.

Retailers can implement a fair-pricing strategy by clearing two hurdles. First, they must make the cultural and strategic transition from thinking value equals price to realizing that value is the total customer experience. Second, they must understand the principles of fair pricing and muster the courage needed to put them into practice. Retailers who price fairly sell most goods at regular but competitive prices and hold legitimate sales promotions. They make it easy to compare their prices with those of competitors, and they avoid hidden charges. They don't raise prices to take advantage of temporary blips in demand, and they stand behind the products they sell.

Zane's Cycles in Branford, Connecticut, is one of the most successful independent bicycle retailers in the United States. Zane's has grown its one-store business at least 20% every year since it was founded in 1981, selling 4,250 bicycles in 2000 along with a full array of accessories. The company's success illustrates the appeal of fair pricing.

Zane's sells better bike brands with prices starting at $250. It stands behind what it sells with a 30-day test-drive offer (customers can return a bike within 30 days and exchange it for another) and a 90-day price protection guarantee (if a buyer finds the same bike in Connecticut at a lower price within 90 days, Zane's will refund the difference plus 10%). Zane's also offers free lifetime service on all new bicycles it sells; it was likely the first bicycle retailer in the United States to take this step. The promise of lifetime service includes annual tune-ups, brake and gear adjustments, wheel straightening, and more.

Zane's holds only one promotional sale a year, a three-day spring weekend event featuring discounts on all products. Vendors and former employees come to work at the huge event—some even fly in to participate. Customers who purchase a bicycle at Zane's within 90 days before the sale are encouraged to return during the event for a refund based on the discounted price of their bike. The company refunded about $3,000 during the 2000 sale, but most of that money remained in the store because customers bought more gear. Zane's sold 560 bicycles during the 2000 sale— that's more than the typical one-store U.S. bicycle retailer sells in an entire year. And yet the limited dura-

Constant sales, markdowns on overinflated prices, and other forms of pressure pricing may boost sales in the short term. But winning customers' trust through fair pricing will pay off in the long term.

tion of the sale means that Zane's sells about 85% of its bicycles at the regular price.

When Connecticut passed a bike-helmet law in 1992, Zane's sold helmets to kids at cost rather than take advantage of legislated demand. Owner Chris Zane convinced area school administrators to distribute flyers to students under 12 announcing that policy. "We sold a ton of helmets and made a lot of new friends for the store," Zane says. "Our customers trust us. They come in and say, 'I am here to get a bike. What do I need?' They have confidence in our ability to find them just the right bike at a fair price and to stand behind what we sell."

Constant sales, markdowns on overinflated prices, and other forms of pressure pricing may boost sales in the short term. Winning customers' trust through fair pricing will pay off in the long term.

Pillar 5: Save Your Customers' Time

Many consumers are poor in at least one respect: they lack time. Retailers often contribute to the problem by wasting consumers' time and energy in myriad ways, from confusing store layouts to inefficient checkout operations to inconvenient hours of business. When shopping is inconvenient, the value of a retailer's offerings plummets.

Slow checkout is particularly annoying to busy people. Managers usually know how much money they are saving by closing a checkout lane; but they may not realize how many customers they've lost in the process. For a food shopper waiting behind six other customers in the "10 Items or Fewer" lane to buy a carton of milk, the time invested in the purchase may outweigh the value of the milk. The shopper may follow through this time but find another store next time. Studies by America's Research Group, a consumer research company based in Charleston, South Carolina, indicate that 83% of women and 91% of men have ceased shopping at a particular store because of long checkout lines.

To compete most effectively, retailers must offer convenience in four ways. They must offer convenient retail locations and operating hours and be easily available by telephone and the Internet (access convenience). They must make it easy for consumers to identify and select desired products (search convenience). They need to make it possible for people to get the products they want by maintaining a high rate of in-stock items and by delivering store, Internet, or catalog orders swiftly (possession convenience). And they need to let consumers complete or amend transactions quickly and easily (transaction convenience).

ShopKo, a discount chain based in Green Bay, Wisconsin, illustrates how shopping speed and ease can create value. ShopKo's more than 160 large discount stores operate in 19 midwestern, mountain, and northwestern states; 80% of the customer base is working women. With fiscal 1999 sales of $3.9 billion (including its small-market subsidiary, Pamida), ShopKo is much smaller than Wal-Mart, Kmart, or Target, yet it competes successfully against all three. Since 1995, following the arrival of new management a year earlier, ShopKo has more than doubled sales and achieved record earnings growth.

ShopKo takes possession convenience seriously and is in-stock 98% of the time on advertised and basic merchandise. Search convenience is another strength. ShopKo stores are remarkably clean and neat. Major traffic aisles are free of passage-blocking displays. Customers near the front of the store have clear sight lines to the back. Navigational signs hanging from the ceiling and on the ends of the aisles help point shoppers in the right direction. Clothing on a hanger has a size tag on the hanger neck; folded apparel has an adhesive strip indicating the size on the front of the garment. Children's garments have "simple sizing"—extra small, small, medium, and large—with posted signs educating shoppers on how to select the proper size.

ShopKo has a "one-plus-one" checkout policy of opening another checkout lane whenever two customers are waiting in any lane. Ready-to-assemble furniture is sold on a pull-tag system. The customer presents a coded tag at checkout and within three minutes the boxed merchandise is ready to be delivered to the customer's car. These ways of operating give ShopKo an edge in transaction convenience.

ShopKo is succeeding in the fiercely competitive discount sector by focusing on the total shopping experience rather than on having the lowest prices. Shopping speed and ease combined with a pleasant store atmosphere, a well-trained staff, and a carefully selected range of merchandise creates a strong mix of customer value.

While ShopKo creates real convenience for its customers, the term is often used carelessly in retailing. Consider that Internet shopping is commonly referred to as convenient. The Internet does indeed offer superior convenience for some stages of the shopping experience; it is inferior for other stages. On-line shoppers who save a trip to a physical store must wait for delivery. Christmas shoppers who receive gifts ordered on-line *after* the holiday learn a lesson about possession inconvenience. This is one reason that the most promising path for most retailers is a strategy that combines physical and virtual stores. Increasingly, the best-managed retailers will enable customers to take advantage of the most effective features of physical and virtual shopping, even for the same transaction.

Retail competition has never been more intense or more diverse than it is today. Yet the companies featured in this article, and hundreds of other excellent retailers, are thriving. They understand that neither technology nor promises of "the lowest prices anywhere" can substitute for a passionate focus on the total customer experience. These retailers enable customers to solve important problems, capitalize on the power of respectfulness, connect with customers' emotions, emphasize fair pricing, and save customers time and energy. In an age that demands instant solutions, it's not possible to combine those ingredients with Redi-Mix, crank out a concrete-block building, and hope the structure will stand. But retailers who thoughtfully and painstakingly erect these pillars will have a solid operation that is capable of earning customers' business, trust, and loyalty.

Originally published in April 2001
Reprint R0104J

Want to Perfect Your Company's Service? Use Behavioral Science

RICHARD B. CHASE AND SRIRAM DASU

Executive Summary

IT MAY SEEM LIKE the topic of service management has been exhausted. Legions of scholars and practitioners have applied queuing theory to bank lines, measured response times to the millisecond, and created cults around "delighting the customer." But practitioners haven't carefully considered the underlying psychology of service encounters—the feelings that customers experience during these encounters, feelings often so subtle they probably couldn't be put into words.

Fortunately, behavioral science offers new insights into better service management. In this article, the authors translate findings from behavioral-science research into five operating principles. First, finish strong: the ending is far more important that the beginning of an encounter because it's what remains in the customer's memory. Second, get the bad experiences out of the way early: in a

series of events, people prefer to have undesirable
events come first and to have desirable events come last.
Third, segment the pleasure, combine the pain: since
experiences seem longer when they are broken into segments, it's best to combine all the boring or unpleasant
steps of a process into one. Fourth, build commitment
through choice: people are happier when they believe
they have some control over a process, particularly an
uncomfortable one. And fifth, give people rituals and
stick to them: most service-encounter designers don't realize just how ritualistic people are.

Ultimately, only one thing really matters in a service
encounter—the customer's perception of what occurred.
This article will help you engineer your service encounters to enhance your customer's experiences during the
process as well as their recollections of the process after
it is completed.

W HAT DON'T WE KNOW about service manage-
ment? For the past 15 years, legions of scholars and practitioners have studied the subject. They've applied queuing theory to bank lines. They've deified well-run call
centers. They've measured response times to the tenth
decimal point. They've built cults around "moments of
truth," "service recovery," and "delighting the customer."

It may appear, then, that no stone in the service-man-
agement garden has been left unturned, not to mention
analyzed, polished, and replaced. Surprisingly little time,
however, has been spent examining service encounters
from the customer's point of view. Specifically, practitioners haven't carefully considered the underlying psychology of service encounters—the feelings that cus-

tomers experience during these encounters, feelings so subtle they probably couldn't be put into words.

Fortunately, behavioral science offers new insights into better service management. For decades, behavioral and cognitive scientists have studied how people experience social interactions, form judgments, and store memories—as well as what biases they bring to bear on daily life. Their findings hold important lessons for the executives who design and manage service encounters. First, the research tells us a lot about how customers experience the passage of time: when time seems to drag, when it speeds by, and when in a sequence of events an uncomfortable experience will be least noticeable. Second, it helps us understand how customers interpret an event after it's over. For example, people seem to be hardwired to blame an individual rather than a poorly designed system when something goes wrong.

In any service encounter—from a simple pizza pickup to a complex, long-term consulting engagement—perception is reality.

In this article, we'll translate findings from behavioral-science research into operating principles for service-encounter management. And we'll show how managers can optimize those extraordinarily important moments when the company touches its customers—for better and for worse.

Applied Behavioral Science

In any service encounter—from a simple pizza pickup to a complex, long-term consulting engagement—perception is reality. That is, what really matters is how the customer interprets the encounter. Behavioral science can shed light on the complex processes involved in the formation of those perceptions. In particular, it can help managers understand how people react to the sequence and duration of events, and how they rationalize experiences after they occur.

SEQUENCE EFFECTS

According to behavioral scientists, when people recall an experience, they don't remember every single moment of it (unless the experience was short and traumatic). Instead, they recall a few significant moments vividly and gloss over the others—they remember snapshots, not movies. And they carry away an overall assessment of the experience that's based on three factors: the trend in the sequence of pain or pleasure, the high and low points, and the ending.

Not surprisingly, people prefer a sequence of experiences that improve over time. When gambling, they prefer to lose $10 first, then win $5, rather than win $5, then lose $10. There is also evidence that people pay attention to the rate of improvement in a sequence—clearly preferring ones that improve faster. And, most intriguing, the ending matters enormously. (See "End on an Uptick" at the end of this article.) A terrible ending usually dominates a person's recollection of an experience.

DURATION EFFECTS

Psychologists and cognitive scientists have poured enormous effort into unraveling the mysteries of how people process time. When do they pay attention to the passage of time, and how do they estimate its duration? Although much of the mystery still remains, one finding that's been verified repeatedly is that people who are mentally engaged in a task don't notice how long it takes. Another is that, when prompted to pay attention to the passage of time, people overestimate the time elapsed. A third finding is that increasing the number of segments in an encounter lengthens its perceived duration. For example, a ten-minute dance sequence consisting of four segments will seem longer than one identical in length but split into two segments.

Since perceptions of time's passage are so subjective, the obvious question is, When does duration matter? Research indicates that unless an activity is much longer or much shorter than expected, people pay little attention to its duration. There are two reasons for this. First, the pleasurable content of the experience and how it is arranged—rather than how long it takes—seem to dominate people's assessments. And second, aside from one-off transactions such as buying a cup of coffee, service encounters are rarely identical in length, so people have only general reference points for evaluating duration. Their estimates of how long it will take to visit a tax accountant—or go to a ball game, or have minor surgery—are likely to be fuzzy.

RATIONALIZATION EFFECTS

People desperately want things to make sense; if there's no handy explanation for an unexpected event, they'll concoct one. Behavioral scientists call this "counterfactual thinking," but it's simpler to call it second-guessing.

People second-guess because they want one clear reason for why something happened. In their mental simulation, they try to capture the specific what-ifs: "If only *x* hadn't happened, things would be different." Three characteristics stand out in this simulation. First, they view the likely cause as a discrete thing, not a continuous, intertwined process. For example, people are more likely to blame a missed plane on "the backup in the tunnel" than on a cluster of events that—in conjunction—caused their late arrival. Second, people often conclude that deviations from rituals and norms caused the unexpected outcome. Professional sports are loaded with players who follow rituals religiously: some baseball players avoid stepping on the foul line at all costs, and many basketball players have particular dribbling routines before shooting a free throw. Third, people tend to ascribe credit or blame to individuals, not systems. Even when they clearly see that the computer system caused the hotel bill error, for example, they tend to blame the clerk. They want to put a human face on the problem. One final note about ascribing blame: people are far less apt to "search for the guilty" if they think they've had some control over the process that occurred. The more empowered and engaged they feel, the less angry they are when something goes wrong.

In summary, people want explanations, and they'll make them up if they have to. The explanation will nearly always focus on something they can observe—something that is discrete and concrete enough to be changed in their if-only fantasies.

Several operating principles for service-encounter management emerge from the behavioral-science findings we've just reviewed. (For an example of these principles in action, see "Why Cruises Work.")

Principle 1: Finish Strong

Most service providers believe that the beginning and end of an encounter—the so-called service bookends—

are equally weighted in the eyes of the customer. They're dead wrong. The end is far more important because it's what remains in the customer's recollections. Sure, it's important to achieve a base level of satisfactory performance at the beginning, but a company is better off with a relatively weak start and a modest upswing at the end than with a boffo start and a so-so ending.

People's innate preference for improvement is another factor in this principle. We believe that the desire for improvement applies not only to lengthy encounters but also to short, technology-mediated encounters, such as on a Web site. The fact is, very few Web designers have thought this issue through. Most companies spare no expense to make their home pages attractive; a great deal of thought goes into questions of aesthetics, content, and navigation in the top page or two. This is an eminently logical strategy, given the need to get people to enter and engage with the site. However, too many Web encounters start strong then go downhill fast. Our cursory review of commercial Web sites uncovered an alarming number of

Why Cruises Work

Modern cruise lines apply many of the operating principles suggested by behavioral science.

Principle	What Cruise Lines Do
Finish strong	*End each day on a high note with raffles, contests, shows, and so on.*
	End the cruise with the captain's dinner.
	Pass out keepsakes or bottles of wine upon reaching home port.
Segment the pleasure	*Pack many events into one short vacation.*
Create rituals	*Offer captain's dinner and midnight buffets.*

problems: difficulty in exiting the site if an item is out of stock; difficulty in canceling an order if the shipping charges are too high; no notification of security for credit card information, and so on. Make no mistake, the frustrated customer remembers the messy final experience far more clearly than the jazzy, supposedly sticky home page.

That which applies to short encounters goes double for longer service encounters like consulting projects. While it often makes sense to pick low-hanging fruit at the outset, a consultant would be well advised (other things being equal) to schedule the project so that a golden nugget or two appear at the end of the engagement. For instance, a consultant that's hired to reengineer a company's business processes might start with the distribution center and move to the call center later in the project, because he knows from past experience that the call center changes will likely reap a windfall of savings. What you don't want is to have the project results become less and less impressive, even if (as is often the case) its labor costs are following a staged decline. Even though one large consulting firm had performed admirably in its yearlong reengineering project, for example, it received low marks from its client. The consultants achieved more than the goals set, but the lack of a visible upswing in results at the end left the impression of mediocrity. As it turns out, last impressions—not first impressions—endure.

Compare that with another consulting project that ended quite naturally on a high note. A statistician colleague of ours was hired to determine what factors accounted for the sales success of a new video game. The client agreed at the start that the project would be a success if the consultant's model could explain just 6% of the variability in sales among a dozen competing video games. The consultant made progress over the first three months of the project, but it wasn't until the last day of the schedule that the analysis yielded a three-factor combination that explained more than 90% of the variability in sales. (For the gamers out there, these factors were kid testing, advertising, and the number of outlets they could get the game into.) This positive surprise had far more impact than it would have had at the outset, since the clients' longer-term involvement had sensitized them to the complexity of the task. Our colleague was lucky to deliver such a clear, better-than-anticipated result; he was luckier still to have done so at the eleventh hour.

Even if you can't end with a substantive bang, it's smart to finish with a stylistic flourish. Consider the airline industry, which suffers from high levels of customer dissatisfaction due to flight delays and cancellations, inadequate legroom, and lost luggage. Without a doubt, those failures have to be addressed. But we'd guess that airlines could make up some ground if they paid more attention to their customers' last encounter—baggage collection. Why not offer a new service—aides to help passengers in the baggage claim area? Simply having someone there would show concern for passengers.

Malaysian Airlines is one of the few carriers that understands that the encounter isn't over when the customer steps off the plane. Several years ago, an acquaintance was traveling by Malaysian Airlines with her nine-month-old son. Even after nine years, she fondly recalls the help that the flight attendants gave her with baggage collection and ground transportation. It cost the airline little to provide that end-of-encounter assistance—and it gained a loyal customer who's described that experience to fellow travelers dozens of times since. As simple as that example sounds, such small touches have a disproportionate effect on customers' recollections.

Principle 2: Get the Bad Experiences Out of the Way Early

Behavioral science tells us that, in a sequence of events involving good and bad outcomes, people prefer to have undesirable events come first—so they can avoid dread—and to have desirable events come at the end of a sequence—so they can savor them.

This principle has concrete, immediate implications for how health care professionals manage their encounters with patients. Imagine Danielle, a pediatric dental hygienist, who has almost finished cleaning Asher's teeth. Asher, a skittish six-year-old and a frequent visitor to the clinic, suffers from a mild form of gingivitis and has several cavities. Danielle accidentally scrapes a particularly sensitive spot, causing the boy momentary pain. She still needs to clean two more teeth, which she is sure are not as sensitive. She could either end the cleaning now and resume on the next visit, or she could complete it today. Continuing would subject Asher to more discomfort, although it would be significantly less than what he just felt. She is also wondering whether continuing (hence, increasing the total pain) will affect Asher's perception of the cleaning experience and his behavior on subsequent visits.

According to behavioral research, Danielle should finish the job. Asher will carry away a better memory. He will remember the treatment, of course, but also that the pain "wasn't so bad at the end." Danielle will have extended a painful experience, yet because the ending was slightly less painful, Asher's overall assessment of it will improve.

Most companies' services don't cause physical pain, obviously. And often the discomfort that's part of a service encounter occurs early naturally: the wait in line (unpleasant) comes before the meal or the theme park ride (pleasant). When that's not the case, it may be necessary to extend the encounter to soften the ending experience.

In professional services, the unpleasantness often comes in the form of bad news. Most people want bad news brought to their attention right away. Unfortunately, service providers are human just like the rest of us—they dread delivering bad news, so they delay it until the last possible moment. This is exactly the wrong thing to do. Get bad news, pain, discomfort, long waits in line, and other unpleasant things out of the way as soon as possible so they don't dominate the customer's recollection of the entire experience.

Principle 3: Segment the Pleasure, Combine the Pain

As we noted earlier, experiences seem longer when they are broken into segments. In addition, people have an asymmetric reaction to losses and gains. Compare winning $10 in one gamble with winning $5 twice. Most of us would prefer to win twice. What about losing $10 in one game as compared with losing $5 in each of two gambles? Here, most people prefer only one loss. That's why companies should break pleasant experiences into multiple stages and combine unpleasant ones into a single stage.

Not many businesses have grasped this notion. Health care facilities, for example, typically make patients wait at multiple points before they see the physician, but doing so makes the overall wait appear even longer. Clinics would do better to let patients spend more time in the waiting room so they don't have to endure a second, third, or fourth wait in the examining rooms.

Phone help-line menus are frustrating in a similar way. To reach the department that can resolve a problem, a customer must listen to instructions and press (or voice) a response. It often takes four or five such steps to get to the right place. Even if the actual time required to run through, say, four menu queries is less than to run through two, people recall four as taking longer. Service companies would do well to cut the number of steps it takes to reach the final destination, thereby reducing the perceived pain of waiting.

The best trade shows have grasped both halves of this principle. They combine as many of the boring paperwork steps as possible. The Internet World trade show, for example, lets attendees preregister over the Internet. When they arrive, they simply pick up a badge that's been programmed with personal data. The badges allow them to get information at any booth—attendees just swipe them through a reading device, thus avoiding an endless exchange of business cards and sign-in sheets. The things that attendees enjoy and come to see, such as product demos, are plentiful, and they're spread throughout the conference.

Disney's theme parks also understand both halves of the principle. They do a great job of distracting customers who are waiting in line, thus lessening their discomfort. And they make the rides really short, as well. That's done primarily so that more people can get on them, but this efficiency has the added benefit of segmenting the pleasure, which in turn creates the perception of a longer and richer day at the theme park. From the customer's point of view, two 90-second rides last longer than one three-minute ride.

Principle 4: Build Commitment Through Choice

A fascinating study found that blood donors perceived significantly less discomfort when they were allowed to select the arm from which the blood would be drawn.[1] The lesson is clear: people are happier and more comfortable when they believe they have some control over a process, particularly an uncomfortable one. Often the control handed over is largely symbolic (as in the choice of arm). In other cases, it's very real: the medical profession has long recognized the value of allowing the patient to make an informed choice about alternative treatments for cancer and heart disease. These are extremely important, high-stakes decisions, and great value is gained by including the patient in the decision. He or she feels less helpless, less hopeless, and more committed to making the process work.

Many companies have learned to apply this principle in less life-threatening situations. Several airlines, for example, let passengers choose when they want to have their meal served during long flights. Most hotels give customers a choice of using an alarm clock or receiving a wake-up call. And some banks have moved away from snake line configurations and back to individual lines so that customers can work with their favorite teller.

As one Midwestern company learned, this principle can both save money and make clients happy. Customers were complaining to the Xerox machine-servicing company that repairs didn't happen quickly enough. At first, the company considered adding more repair personnel, but upon reflection, it decided to give customers more choice over the schedule. It let them determine the urgency of the problem—service people would arrive faster for a critical failure than for a less urgent one. As expected, this improved customer satisfaction, but what surprised the company was that fewer repair people were needed. The change also reduced the turnover of customer service reps because there were fewer scheduling conflicts with the customers. Conventional wisdom would say that allowing customers to pick the time would force the company to hire more staff. Here, however, as is often the case, customers actually wanted choice more than they wanted an instantaneous response.

Principle 5: Give People Rituals, and Stick to Them

Most service-encounter designers don't realize just how ritualistic people are. They find comfort, order, and meaning in repetitive, familiar activities. Rituals are particularly important in longer-term, professional-service encounters: they're used to mark key moments in the relationship, establish professional credentials, create a feeling of inclusion, flatter customers, set expectations, and get feedback. Common rituals include glowing introductions of staff at the start of an engagement, kickoff dinners, elegant PowerPoint presentations, final celebrations, and formal presentations to the CEO (even though he or she may not have an interest in the project). Many rituals are so small in scale that they're hard to name.

Nonetheless, they play an important part in customers' perceptions of the experience. When McKinsey consultants listen to clients, for example, they pepper pauses in the conversation with a characteristic, noncommittal "uh-huh, uh-huh" that somebody once labeled the "McKinsey grunt." Sounds silly, but clients notice when it's missing.

Behavioral researchers have observed that these rituals provide an implicit standard for evaluating service encounters. Deviation from them is often cited as the cause of a failure—particularly in professional services, where customers have difficulty evaluating precise causes and effects. Check in with customers after something's gone badly with a service engagement, and you'll find that this is quite true. "If Henry had covered the ten-step model on the new benefits system like Susan did for the old one, it wouldn't have flopped." (The new system didn't require the ten-step ritual; it failed for a constellation of other reasons.) Or, "The consultant wearing the string tie was off in his forecast by 10%." (The dress code violation had nothing to do with the consultant's technical skills.)

It's easy to laugh at those examples, and more generally to dismiss people's tendency to focus on deviations from norms and rituals when they're trying to explain a failure. But make no mistake, behavioral science clearly shows how critical rituals are in long-term relationships. Not getting the weekly call from the consultant on a project, not copying the CEO on a progress report, not returning phone calls immediately—any of these lapses can be blamed after the fact for a failure. They can also, and even more ominously, shift a customer's perceptions about the quality of the service, the service providers, and the company they represent.

Ultimately, only one thing really matters in a service encounter—the customer's perceptions of what occurred. Executives who design and oversee service encounters need to focus far more of their attention on the underlying factors affecting those perceptions. We believe that service encounters can be engineered to enhance the customer's experience during the process and his or her recollection of the process after it is completed.

We've used science to explore those factors, but you'll need to use your imagination to bring them alive. Put yourself in your customers' shoes and imagine their journey. Visualize every moment they spend with you and your employees. Which of their encounters should be lengthened? Which should be shortened? Where in a process are distractions most effective? Where should you offer choice to the customer? Which process rituals should not be violated? What are the last images of your service that customers take away, and how can you enhance them?

Behavioral science, applied with equal doses of empathy and imagination, can improve service delivery. More important, it can change the impressions that your customers remember, refer back to, and pass on to future customers.

End on an Uptick

DANIEL KAHNEMAN, a professor of psychology at Princeton University, is a leading researcher in cognitive psychology. In a 1993 experiment, he and his colleagues asked subjects to choose between two unpleasant experiences. In the first, subjects immersed their hands in uncomfortably cool water (57° F) for 60 seconds. In the second, the same subjects immersed their hand in cool water (57° F) for 60 seconds followed by 30 seconds in slightly warmer water (59° F). Even though the second sequence extended the total discomfort time, when subjects were asked which experience they would repeat, nearly 70% chose the second one.

Kahneman found similar results in a field experiment he performed with D.A. Redelmeier. They learned that prolonging a colonoscopy by leaving the colonoscope in place for about a minute after the procedure was completed—thus decreasing the level of discomfort for the final moments of the procedure—produced significant improvements in patients' perceptions of the experience.

The Right Remedy

HOW DO YOU MAKE UP for a service-encounter error? Research on what customers perceive as a fair remedy suggests that the answer depends on whether it is an outcome error or a process error. A botched task calls for material compensation, while poor treatment from a server calls for an apology. Reversing these recovery actions is unlikely to be effective.

Imagine being a copy store manager faced with two complaining customers. One says that the job was done right but the clerk was surly. The other says that the clerk was pleasant but when he got home, he realized that his report was missing two pages, and he had to take it to a competitor near his house to get the job done right. What should you do? In the case of the rude clerk, don't give the customer some tangible compensation, such as a coupon for his next visit. All the customer really wants is a sincere apology from the clerk and the manager. In the case of the botched job, you can apologize all over the place, but that won't satisfy the customer. He wants the job done right, and he wants some compensation for his inconvenience. Thus, while apologies are appropriate in both situations, behavioral research clearly indicates that process-based remedies should be applied to process-based problems and outcome-based remedies should be applied to outcome-based problems.

Note

1. R.T. Mills and D.S. Krantz, "Information, Choice, and Reactions to Stress: A Field Experiment in a Blood Bank with Laboratory Analogue," *Journal of Personality and Social Psychology*, 1979.

Originally published in June 2001
Reprint R0106D

Don't Homogenize, Synchronize

MOHANBIR SAWHNEY

Executive Summary

TO BE MORE RESPONSIVE to customers, companies often break down organizational walls between their units—setting up all manner of cross-business and cross-functional task forces and working groups and promoting a "one-company" culture. But such attempts can backfire terribly by distracting business and functional units and by contaminating their strategies and processes.

Fortunately, there's a better way, says the author. Rather than tear down organizational walls, a company can make them permeable to information. It can synchronize all its data on products, filtering the information through linked databases and applications and delivering it in a coordinated, meaningful form to customers. As a result, the organization can present a single, unified face to the customer—one that can change

85

as market conditions warrant—without imposing homogeneity on its people. Such synchronization can lead
not just to stronger customer relationships and more
sales but also to greater operational efficiency. It
allows a company, for example, to avoid the high
costs of maintaining many different information systems
with redundant data.

The decoupling of product control from customer control in a synchronized company reflects a fundamental
fact about business: While companies have to focus on
creating great products, customers think in terms of the
activities they perform and the benefits they seek. For
companies, products are ends, but for customers, products are means. The disconnect between how customers
think and how companies organize themselves is what
leads to inefficiencies and missed opportunities, and
that's exactly the problem that synchronization solves.
Synchronized companies can get closer to customers,
sustain product innovation, and improve operational efficiency—goals that have traditionally been very difficult to
achieve simultaneously.

STEP INSIDE THE corporate headquarters of Palm in
Santa Clara, California, and the first thing you're likely to
notice is a large poster of the defining feature of the company's handheld computers: the HotSync button. If
you're a Palm user, you know that dropping the handheld into its docking cradle and pressing the HotSync
button allows you to effortlessly and seamlessly synchronize it with your desktop computer. In a matter of
seconds, the boundaries between the two data silos dis-

appear. The poster underscores one of Palm's key inno-
vations and biggest selling points. But it also speaks
volumes about the promise of business technology in
general. Ask yourself this: "Does my company have a
HotSync button?"

Every decent-sized enterprise has many organizational and technological silos. Product lines, business
units, channels, geographies, and IT systems are separated by well-defined and often rigid walls, which dimin-
ish the company's ability to build strong, broad customer
relationships. Because the walls tend to obstruct the flow
of information, different parts of the company can end
up selling to the same customers, sometimes competing
for the same business without even knowing it. Just
think of how your own relationships with companies are
fragmented. If you're an AT&T customer, for instance,
you may have several different relationships with the
company: as a long-distance subscriber, a wireless user, a
cable TV watcher, a cable modem customer, and a credit
card holder. Tracked in five different databases, you
appear to the company as five different customers. The
more decentralized the business, the greater the costs of
such fragmentation. As the number and rigidity of walls
increase, a company will tend to miss more and more
market opportunities.

Executives understand this problem well—they see
and feel its consequences every day. But they often
assume it's a people problem. "If we could just get our
employees to reach out to one another across organizational boundaries," the thinking goes, "we could be
much more responsive to customers and much more
productive in our operations." Though understandable,
this reaction often leads to superficial solutions that

create more problems than they solve. CEOs start to urge—even force—people from different units to work together, setting up all manner of cross-functional and cross-business task forces and teams. They seek to establish companywide processes, to create a single "customer-focused" culture, and to impose uniform performance-measurement and compensation systems. Such moves sound rational—in theory. But in reality, attempts to erase organizational boundaries can be destructive. Different business units have different strategic and product imperatives, and different functions rely on different kinds of employees with different skills and ways of working. Imposing uniformity can blur the organization's focus on product and functional excellence. By trying to optimize cooperation across units, executives end up lowering the performance of each unit.

There's a better way. Rather than tear down organizational walls, you can make them permeable to information. You can synchronize all your company's data on products, filtering it through linked databases and applications and delivering it in a coordinated, meaningful form to customers. As a result, you can present a single, unified face to the customer—a face that can change as market conditions warrant—without imposing organizational homogeneity on your people. Such synchronization can lead not just to stronger customer relationships and hence more sales but also to greater operational efficiency. It allows a company, for example, to avoid the high costs of maintaining many different information systems with redundant data. By creating the equivalent of a HotSync button for your company, you can enhance your market responsiveness while at the same time reducing your costs. (For a look at how a company should synchronize its business, see the exhibit "The Three Dimensions of Synchronization.")

Synchronizing 3M

Consider the recent experience of 3M, a 99-year-old, $15 billion company with an unsurpassed record of innovation. 3M is a study in product diversity, selling more than 50,000 products in 200 countries. If you brought together all the company's branded products that begin with the letter "A" alone, you'd see everything from wallpaper remover and antacid tablets to fiber-optic cable and fire-fighting foam. Much of 3M's success as an innovator can be attributed to its highly decentralized structure: it develops and markets its products through more than 40 different divisions, each of which functions as a separate company, with its own processes, systems, and brands. The organizational diversity has been great for the company, enabling its employees to maintain the deep focus required for breakthrough thinking.

But the fragmentation has been bad for the company's customers. Sales reps from each division traditionally called on customers independently, and each business unit collected its own sales and product information in its own database. As a result, it was impossible for the company to answer a simple but crucial question: How much business do we do with a specific customer? Without knowing the answer, 3M was hamstrung in the market. It could not uncover cross-selling opportunities by comparing same-customer purchase information or by analyzing buying patterns across product categories. It could not even assess how important each customer was to the company as a whole. There was also a huge cost penalty. Each business unit had to maintain and

The Three Dimensions of Synchronization

Synchronization needs to take place along three dimensions: the offerings your company presents to customers, your information systems, and your organization. Each, as indicated here, involves a decoupling of product-focused resources from customer-focused resources.

	Offerings Synchronization	Technology Synchronization	Organization Synchronization
Objective	Provide unified, flexible face to customers	Create IT architecture that bridges organizational silos	Be responsible to customers while maintaining product and functional excellence
Decoupling	Decouple customer offering from individual products	Decouple customer-facing applications from back-end infrastructure	Decouple customer expertise from product and functional expertise
Key Enablers	Customer activity blueprint; integrated customer and product databases	Tiered architecture with middleware layer that coordinates and integrates	Centralized shared services units; product units as "suppliers" to customer-facing teams
Outcome	Integrated and flexible offerings aligned with customer activities	Integrated and flexible IT architecture with modular components	Integrated shared services organization, product organization, and customer organization
Challenges	Gaining deep contextual understanding of customer activities	Integrating diverse legacy applications, databases, and computer systems	Managing change, redesigning incentives

update its customer database separately—a mammoth, duplicative task that was not only expensive but also highly prone to error. In fact, 40% of the customer records in 3M's various U.S. databases had invalid addresses.

The same problems arose when the company moved onto the Internet. Decentralized and poorly coordinated, 3M's Web sites mirrored the structure of the company itself, with customers having to visit several different sites to get information on related products. A health care professional, for instance, might buy products and services from 3M's pharmaceutical division, skin health division, medical-surgical division, medical specialties division, and office supplies division. To get information about these products, she would have to register separately with each of these divisions' Web sites, receiving a different password and user ID, and she would have to familiarize herself with the sites' different designs and navigation schemes. When she bought something from one unit, moreover, no record of that transaction would be available to any other unit, which made it impossible for her to receive fast, consistent customer service from the company. In short, 3M was out of sync. It presented many different and often contradictory faces to its markets, all of them reflecting its internal silos rather than its customers' needs.

In 1997, the company decided to fix the problem—not by imposing uniformity on its organization but through a $20 million initiative to create a global data warehouse to store customer, product, sales, inventory, and financial information across all product divisions and geographies. Now up and running, the integrated database tracks 250,000 customer relationships and 500,000 product configurations. It is accessible through an easy-to-use Web interface, featuring a single registration procedure and password, powerful search and product-recommendation engines, and a consistent look and feel. Employees and partners can tap into the system from their desktop computers and quickly find up-to-date information on product prices, availability, and specifications as well as detailed summaries of each customer account. Customer profitability, product profitability, and partner performance can now be analyzed across the entire company, helping 3M allocate its corporate resources more adroitly.

Synchronization has allowed 3M to present a unified face to its customers. Equally important, though, it has enabled the company to present new faces to its customers, quickly and seamlessly. With customer relationships and product configurations now stored in a single database, the company can redesign, reaggregate, and reconfigure its offerings to better fulfill the needs of groups of customers or to capitalize on market opportunities. On the Web, for example, the company now offers ten "customer centers" aimed at particular segments of buyers. These customer centers, which include Health Care, Home & Leisure, Graphic Arts, Architecture & Construction, and Office, pull together all relevant products and services from across the entire 3M organization. The centers are often further subdivided to focus on even narrower market segments. Customers visiting the Health Care center, for instance, can choose from an area for health care professionals, which offers products and services for doctors, dentists, nurses, and information managers; an area for consumers, which offers information on products and services for personal health care; and an area for manufacturers, which showcases technologies and products that 3M offers to producers of cosmetics, pharmaceuticals, and baby products.

3M's wares are no longer presented silo by silo—even though the goods are still developed by discrete product units with the focus and autonomy required to be highly innovative. Through synchronization, 3M has tapped into what I call the *eBay effect*, after the dominant on-line auction house. By manipulating information stored in its databases, eBay has long been able to rapidly redesign the way it appears to customers. Think for a moment about what happened on the eBay site on January 14, 1999, the day after Michael Jordan announced his retirement from the Chicago Bulls. That morning, eBay announced the opening of a brand new storefront devoted entirely to Michael Jordan memorabilia. The products on display ranged from Jordan's 1986 Fleer rookie card to autographed game jerseys to Upper Deck's famous "Last Shot," a photograph showing Jordan sinking the final basket in a Bulls victory. By rolling out a new bundle of products, eBay created, in effect, a new version of itself, tailored especially for Jordan's myriad fans. And that was not an isolated event—the company sets up new storefronts nearly every day as market opportunities arise.

As 3M's experience shows, the eBay effect is not limited to Internet outfits. It can be replicated by any company. Whether you're selling through the Web, a sales force, a phone center, or almost any other channel, you can use synchronized product and customer data to tailor product sets and marketing pitches to individual customers or customer segments. You can slice and dice your product lines to create targeted bundles that you've never offered—or even thought about offering—before.

Rewiring Thomson Financial

Gaining that capability, as we've seen, requires a company to separate control over products from control over product and customer information; the former can remain fragmented among product units, but the latter needs to be consolidated and coordinated at the points of customer contact. But there's more to it than that. Synchronization also requires a new approach to information technology. In most companies, individual product and geographic units maintain many of their own integrated information systems, encompassing both a basic infrastructure of databases and networking protocols and a set of so-called customer-facing applications—software programs, such as ordering systems, used either by frontline personnel interacting with customers or by customers themselves. By fragmenting control over the customer-facing applications, this practice forces companies to go to market with an uncoordinated set of products. To make synchronization work, the customer-facing applications have to be decoupled from the back-end IT infrastructure—just as product information is decoupled from product development.

Look, for example, at the way in which Thomson Financial, a $2 billion provider of electronic information to the worldwide financial industry, went about synchronizing its business. A subsidiary of the Thomson Corporation, Thomson Financial was founded in 1980 and over the next two decades grew into a vast, loosely knit portfolio of small- and medium-sized business units that sold different but often closely related information products. By 1998, the company had 40 executives with the title of president or CEO, some running businesses with less than $5 million in revenues, and the various units offered thousands of products to overlapping customer bases. It was not uncommon for a major customer like Merrill Lynch to be besieged by over 30 different Thomson salespeople and to have to sort through information from 37 different systems and 23 different data sets. And despite several market-leading products, like First Call, Datastream, I/B/E/S, Portia, and AutEx, brand awareness for Thomson Financial was poor.

The fragmentation was becoming a severe liability for Thomson Financial. Intense competition was turning many of the company's products into commodities, placing increasing pressure on margins. For example, company research reports, which had been sold at a premium price by Thomson units First Call and Investext, were being offered at a fraction of the cost by competitors like Multex. Worse yet, Reuters and Bloomberg were giving away research reports as part of broader service offerings. Unable to bundle its products into value-added packages, Thomson had little to distinguish itself in the increasingly price-competitive marketplace. At the same time, its customers were getting fed up with the lack of consistency in dealing with the company. They were demanding greater standardization, integration, and personalization of the company's entire product line.

In response to the mounting market pressures, Dick Harrington, the CEO of Thomson Corporation, and Pat Tierney, the CEO of Thomson Financial, launched an effort to reinvent the company. Their goal was to transform Thomson Financial from a product-centric company, which found customers for its products, to a customer-centric company, which would find products for its customers. To accomplish this shift, Thomson Financial synchronized its formerly fragmented electronic products, enabling it to create flexible new offerings tailored to the needs of different customers, and it revamped its information architecture to support this new way of going to market.

The company began by identifying and profiling its three major customer segments: portfolio managers who manage money for clients, equity analysts who research stocks and bonds, and traders who buy and sell financial instruments. Thomson analyzed the work flows of each segment to come up with a detailed map of customer activities. The activities of a portfolio manager, for example, included researching stocks, placing trades, tracking settlements, tallying portfolio values, reporting results to customers and other institutions, and evaluating performance. Thomson then overlaid its products and services onto the customer activity map, revealing how they supported the various activities. This exercise allowed the company to see how its products could be assembled into flexible new sets that would meet the broad needs of the three customer segments, providing the basis for the design of customized desktop-computer interfaces for each segment. (For more on how the company reconfigured its product lines, see the exhibit "Synchronizing Thomson Financial's Offerings.")

To make this new approach work, Thomson had to find a way to gather all the product and customer information locked up in its business-unit databases and systems, integrate it, and funnel it to the new customer interfaces. It did this by installing software called "middleware." In simple terms, middleware serves as an information translator, taking information from, in Thomson's case, diverse and disbursed legacy applications and delivering it in a consistent, usable form to the new customer-facing applications. Middleware has allowed the company to move from an *integrated architecture,* where each product unit had its own integrated IT infrastructure and applications, to a *tiered architecture,* where control over the back-end infrastructure, including databases and networking protocols, has been separated from control over the customer-facing applications.[1] (For a fuller description of the IT platform, see the exhibit "Thomson Financial's Synchronized IT Architecture.") By dramatically reducing the cost of maintaining existing systems, the new IT architecture is having a profound effect on the way the company allocates its techni-

---

Synchronizing Thomson Financial's Offerings

Thomson Financial traditionally offered its customers a fragmented set of products, each controlled by an isolated business unit. That created confusion and inefficiency. To fix the problem, Thomson synchronized its products, creating a set of tailored offerings for individual customer segments. Here, we see how the company thought through its offerings for portfolio managers. It first analyzed all the discrete activities in a portfolio manager's work flow, from researching individual stocks to measuring overall portfolio performance. It then matched up the products its units produced that supported each activity. By bundling these products together, Thomson now delivers much greater value to these customers—at a much lower cost.

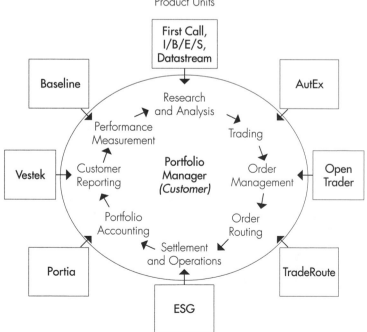

Product Units

cal resources. Jeff Scott, Thomson Financial's chief technology officer, says that his team used to spend 80% of its budget on infrastructure development and maintenance and only 20% on developing and enhancing offerings for

---

Thomson Financial's Synchronized IT Architecture

Thomson Financial has moved from an integrated architecture, where individual units controlled both IT infrastructure and customer-facing applications, to a tiered architecture, when control over the customer-facing applications is consolidated with customer-focused teams. The decoupling of customer-facing applications and back-end infrastructure is made possible by a new application-server layer, called "middleware," which allows legacy applications and products to be represented as "objects" or modular components that can be aggregated and flexibly assembled to create tailored solutions for customers. In addition to creating a tiered architecture, the company has enhanced IT synchronization by developing a common nomenclature for products, common protocols for accessing application components, common XML standards, and common standards for look and feel, and by consolidating its networks and hardware.

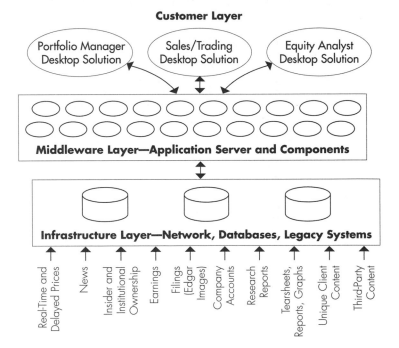

customers. With the new, tiered architecture, he estimates that only 40% of the company's IT resources will
now have to be invested in infrastructure, while 60% will
go to customer-facing applications. This shift will allow
the company to be more responsive to its customers,
bring new offerings to market more quickly, and cross-
sell its products more effectively.

Synchronization is bringing competitive benefits as
well. According to CEO Tierney, Thomson Financial has
been able to effectively fend off "point" competitors—
those that provide single products at low prices—by
offering customers convenient one-stop shopping for a
wide range of products. It has also been able to greatly
expand its market by cross-selling all its products to
70,000 portfolio managers and 10,000 corporations that
used to buy only one or a few Thomson products. And it
has enhanced the value of its corporate brand by putting
a Thomson Financial interface on thousands of customers' desktops.

A More Rational Organization

We've seen how synchronization requires the decoupling
of product information from products themselves and
the decoupling of customer-facing applications from the
basic IT infrastructure. There's also an organizational
decoupling that needs to take place: the separation of
product-focused teams from customer-focused teams.
While individual product units can continue to have
responsibility for product development and production,
they need to cede control over customer relationships to
new groups organized around particular market segments. Although making this organizational change is a
tough challenge, it's one that many large companies are

already pursuing. In a drive to become more customer focused, Motorola and Hewlett-Packard, for example, are attempting to organize their sales organizations and customer service channels around their customers rather than their products.

The most radical change involved in such efforts is getting the product groups to alter their mind-sets. They need to view the internal customer-facing units, rather than the external end users, as their customers. That doesn't mean that they should dismantle all their marketing skills. The expertise of product-based sales forces, for example, often remains highly valuable. At Thomson Financial, the product units continue to maintain sales forces, but they have fewer people and play different roles. In essence, the product salesperson has become a product specialist, providing in-depth technical support to the customer-facing sales teams. And while the customer-facing teams have the authority over customer relationships, the product specialists still assist on an as-needed basis. Ultimately, the compensation of the product specialists should be based on the demand for their products from the customer teams. During a transitional period, however, hybrid compensation systems may be necessary to encourage the participation of the product groups. Thomson Financial currently offers commissions to product specialists on every sale made by the customer teams, ensuring that the specialists do not feel suddenly disenfranchised.

Making the transition from a product-centric sales organization to a customer-centric sales organization will frequently require the development of new skills in customer account management and new measures for customer account potential and profitability. If you can't measure revenues and profits by customer account, you won't be able to reward people for focusing on growing customer accounts instead of just pushing products. You'll send mixed signals to your company, undermining your new structure.

As part of this realignment, companies should also consider consolidating support functions that have traditionally been distributed among the product groups, creating a set of shared services, such as finance, purchasing, and human resources, that support both the customer-facing teams and the product units. The centralization of functions creates economies of scale and builds a critical mass of expertise in core support skills. The activities of all the product and shared-services groups can be coordinated by a corporate core of executives who are responsible for strategy, leadership, and resource allocation. (The exhibit "The Synchronized Organization" provides an overview of this organizational structure.)

The decoupling of product control from customer control in a synchronized company reflects a fundamental fact about business: while companies have to focus on creating great products, customers think in terms of the activities they perform and the benefits they seek. For companies, products are ends, but for customers, products are means. The disjunction between how customers think and how companies organize themselves is what leads to inefficiencies and missed opportunities, and that's exactly the problem that synchronization solves. Synchronized companies are able to get closer to customers, sustain product innovation, and improve operational efficiency—three goals that have traditionally been extraordinarily difficult to achieve simultaneously.

Synchronizing Knowledge at P&G

PRODUCT AND CUSTOMER DATA aren't the only things that tend to be locked up in various organizational silos. Employee knowledge also tends to be fragmented, with one unit's experience and know-how inaccessible to other units. As a result, people are constantly reinventing the wheel, at a very high cost.

The Synchronized Organization

In a synchronized company, control over product development and manufacturing is separate from control over customers. The internal product teams no longer sell directly to end users; rather, they sell their goods to internal customer-facing teams, which have authority over all aspects of customer relationships. Both the product units and the customer teams are served by a set of centralized shared-services groups, such as purchasing, human resources, finance, and information technology. Executive management forms the corporate core, coordinating both the shared services and the product units.

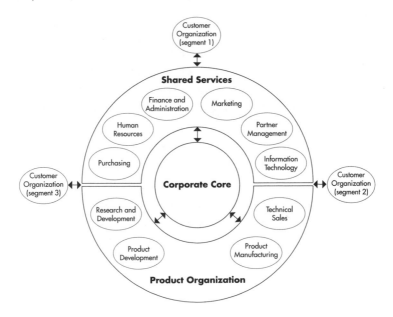

Information technology can be used to synchronize knowledge across even the largest, most dispersed companies. Look, for example, at what Procter & Gamble has done for its marketers. Not long ago, if you were a P&G brand manager in, say, Malaysia, you would have to work largely in isolation from your peers in other locations. If you were looking to create an advertising campaign for a new brand of deodorant, you'd hire a local ad agency, and many weeks and dollars later, the agency would unveil its plan of attack. At that point, you'd have to cross your fingers and hope for the desired results. And you'd feel very frustrated. You'd know that somewhere, sometime, someone in the company probably created a successful campaign for a similar product under similar conditions—but you'd have no efficient way to locate that knowledge.

In 1994, P&G addressed this problem by installing a standardized worldwide ad-testing system. So if you were that Malaysian brand manager today, you wouldn't pick up the phone to call the ad agency; you'd log on to your computer and connect to the system. You'd input basic information about the product category, the market conditions, the competitive context, and the demographic profile of the target audience. You'd answer some questions about market share, the depth of distribution, and the primary sales channels. And finally, you'd enter information about the specifics of the advertising campaign. What's the budget? Is the media print, TV, or radio? Do you think a good approach would be "celebrity endorsement," "man on the street," or "the product as hero"? Based on such inputs, the program would search through every advertisement that the company has ever run, outputting examples that closely match your needs. You might find, for example, that the best model is an advertisement that ran two years ago in Brazil for another personal hygiene product and produced strong results in terms of brand awareness and customer trial. The system would provide you with the video clip of the actual advertisement, the awareness and sales numbers that it generated, and even a set of notes on the contextual differences between the Brazilian campaign and the one you're developing for Malaysia. Synchronizing knowledge in this way saves enormous amounts of time and money—and leads to better performance as well.

Note

1. For a more detailed discussion of the decoupling pattern in networks, see Mohanbir Sawhney and Deval Parikh, "Where Value Lives in a Networked World," *HBR* January 2001.

Originally published in July–August 2001
Reprint R0107G

Firing Up the Front Line

JON R. KATZENBACH AND

JASON A. SANTAMARIA

Executive Summary

FOR MANY ORGANIZATIONS, achieving competitive advantage means eliciting superior performance from employees on the front line—the burger flippers, hotel room cleaners, and baggage handlers whose work has an enormous effect on customers. That's no easy task. Frontline workers are paid low wages, have scant hope of advancement, and—not surprisingly—often care little about the company's performance.

But then how do some companies succeed in engaging the emotional energy of rank-and-file workers? A team of researchers at McKinsey & Company and the Conference Board recently explored that question and discovered that one highly effective route is demonstrated by the U.S. Marine Corps. The Marines' approach to motivation follows the "mission, values, and pride" path, which researchers say is practical and relevant for the business world.

More specifically, the authors say the Marines follow five practices: they overinvest in cultivating core value; prepare every person to lead, including frontline supervisors; learn when to create teams and when to create single-leader work groups; attend to all employees, not just the top half; and encourage self-discipline as a way of building pride.

The authors admit there are critical differences between the Marines and most businesses. But using vivid examples from companies such as KFC and Marriott International, the authors illustrate how the Marines' approach can be translated for corporate use.

Sometimes, the authors maintain, minor changes in a company's standard operating procedure can have a powerful effect on frontline pride and can result in substantial payoffs in company performance.

I<small>F THERE IS ONE CHALLENGE</small> that confounds the many organizations that depend on frontline workers, it is how to engender their emotional energy. That's understandable. Frontline employees are often unskilled and are paid little. Their work can be stubbornly unexciting. They flip burgers, clean hotel bathrooms, answer call-center phones, and unload cargo holds. Because their work is monotonous and their chances for advancement are limited, most frontline employees work for a regular paycheck and nothing more; they never emotionally connect with their employers, let alone care about the company's long-term performance. Yet their impact on the customer's experience—not to mention the company's profits—can be enormous.

It would be a mistake, however, to see frontline employees simply as liabilities to be contained. Many have the potential to contribute substantially to the organization. Marriott International, for instance, boasts of scores of employees and managers drawn from welfare rolls. At first, those workers fit the stereotype of inexperienced, undisciplined newcomers. Now, however, many of them exhibit remarkable performance. This story of engaged, high-performing frontline workers, and others like it at companies as diverse as Toyota and Hill's Pet Nutrition, clearly show that managing the rank and file isn't just a challenge; it's an opportunity.

For the past three years, a team of analysts from McKinsey & Company and the Conference Board, a business research organization, has studied companies known to engage the emotional energy of frontline workers. From an original list of 50 possibilities, 30 companies were selected for close analysis. Some, such as the Home Depot, Southwest Airlines, and KFC, already were well known for their expertise in managing frontline employees. Others, such as Vail Ski and Snowboard School in Colorado and MACtel in Anchorage, Alaska, were less famous but still provided compelling examples of managerial programs, policies, and mechanisms that generated workforce enthusiasm—and results.

Halfway into the research project, it was suggested that the team add to its list an organization that had never crossed its radar screen: the U.S. Marine Corps. At first, our team dismissed the idea. What could the captains of war possibly teach the captains of industry about motivation? But after observing the Marines for three months and conducting close to 100 interviews, the team concluded that the Corps outperformed all other organizations when it came to engaging the hearts and minds of the front line. Our research showed that the Marines did so by using five managerial practices that—although rarely found in the for-profit world—are relevant and applicable to business.

Take training, for example. In a typical business organization, a frontline employee undergoes a brief introduction to company procedures and policies, usually conducted by instructors with little on-the-job experience. The new employee receives a manual that explains rules regarding vacation, maternity leave, and the like. If the company's leaders show up, it is in cameo appearances. In general, the new employee experiences no emotions during this process except anxiety or boredom.

Marine training could not be more different. First, it is long: 12 weeks. Very little of that time, however, is spent on building skills or communicating the Corps' procedures and policies. Instead, training is focused entirely on inculcating the organization's values—honor, courage, and commitment. And it is conducted by the organization's most experienced and talented people, who see the job as both an honor and a challenge.

In addition, the Marines fire up their front line through their unique approaches to developing leaders, managing teams, and handling underperforming members of the rank and file. Finally, the Marines create a high-energy front line by using discipline—but not as you see it in the typical business setting. The Marines use discipline not just to punish, but to spawn a culture of self-control and group-control that bolsters performance and raises pride.

There are, of course, limits to any analogy between the Corps and the corporation. The Marines hire many of their people from disadvantaged backgrounds, rely primarily on nonmonetary rewards, and have to keep their recruits for at least four years. Most businesses look for people from solid backgrounds, rely heavily on cash bonuses, and always have the option of firing poor performers.

Also, the Marines induct recruits into a closed, tightly controlled environment. The boot camps on Parris Island, South Carolina, and in San Diego are sealed off from the outside world and its distractions. Recruits are immersed in the Marine experience in a way that intensifies and accelerates the indoctrination process. Because companies send their troops home at night, they cannot enjoy the benefits of such a rarefied environment.

The Marines follow what we call the "mission, values, and pride" path to a high-performing workforce.

Some might argue that the biggest difference is that businesses have customers, and the Marines don't; the job of the Marines is to defeat an enemy or keep the peace in war-torn areas such as Haiti or Beirut. But the Marines do have important constituents who are very like customers and shareholders: the citizens of the United States and their elected representatives. As the only nonessential part of the armed forces, the Marine Corps—with a budget of $10 billion—must prove its worth every day. But even more important, the front lines of the Marines and the front lines of business strive for precisely the same critical objectives: speed, responsiveness, and flexibility.

Mission, Values, Pride

The Marines follow what we have come to call the "mission, values, and pride" (MVP) path to an emotionally engaged, high-performing workforce. (There is, of course, more than one way to energize frontline employees. For a summary of the paths that our research identified, see the exhibit "One Destination, Five Roads.") The leaders of MVP organizations engage the emotional energy of the front line by building collective pride and mutual trust. To foster collective pride, they often emphasize the company's noble purpose or rich legacy. At KFC headquarters in St. Louis, Missouri, a frequently traveled hallway called the Walk of Leaders is home to mounds of memorabilia commemorating great moments in the company's history, such as the opening of the company's first store and the introduction of new menu items. MVP leaders also generate collective pride by articulating and demonstrating strong shared values. Employees who accept those values develop a powerful sense of "one for all and all for one."

MVP leaders create energy through mutual trust in myriad ways. One way is making sure relationships are nonhierarchical, that work teams share ideas, information, and responsibility for failure or success. Mutual trust is also a result of managers and employees keeping promises. Several years ago, the Home Depot hired a former homemaker to work in an outlet's millwork department—a job that required expertise and technical knowledge. Her managers promised that she would receive all the training required to make her a success if she promised to commit to meeting the needs of the department's customers—demanding contractors who were prone to frequent and unpleasant displays of impatience. Both the management and the employee kept their ends of the bargain. The story has become legendary among Home Depot employees. It resonates with them because it reflects the organization's energizing

One Destination, Five Roads

Not every organization engenders emotional energy in the same way. Our research found that there are five distinct managerial paths that result in committed, high-performing frontline workers. The chart summarizes the characteristics of each path and cites notable examples.

	Emotional energy is generated by:	Frontline employees commit themselves to the organization because:	Organizations that follow this path:
The Mission, Values, and Pride Path	mutual trust, collective pride, and self-discipline	They are proud of its aspirations, accomplishments, and legacy; they share its values.	U.S. Marine Corps, 3M, New York City Ballet
The Process and Metrics Path	transparent performance measures and standards; clear tracking of results	They know what each person is expected to do, how performance is measured, and why it matters.	Johnson Controls, Hill's Pet Nutrition, Toyota
The Entrepreneurial Spirit Path	personal freedom, the opportunity for high earnings, and few rules about behavior; people choose their work activities and take significant personal risks	They are in control of their own destinies; they savor the high-risk, high-reward work environment.	Hambrecht & Quist, BMC Software, Vail Ski and Snowboard School
The Individual Achievement Path	intense respect for individual achievement in an environment with limited emphasis on personal risk and reward	They are recognized mostly for the quality of their individual performance.	FirstUSA, McKinsey & Company, Perot Systems
The Reward and Celebration Path	recognition and celebration of organizational accomplishments	They have fun and enjoy the supportive and highly interactive environment.	Mary Kay, Tupperware

commitment to bonds of honesty between executives and the front line.

Every MVP organization follows this path somewhat differently. While the New York City Ballet emphasizes its rich history—the legacy of George Balanchine's and Lincoln Kirstein's relentless pursuit of perfection—to motivate new dancers, Hewlett-Packard—with the famed HP Way—makes shared values its focus. But underlying the varying techniques are the following five practices, each described with recommendations for companies that might seek to embark on the MVP path to win their own competitive battles.

Practice One: Overinvest at the outset in inculcating core values. When new people come on board, most companies make a point of communicating the organization's values. Some distribute wallet cards or wall plaques; others require employees to attend a speech or view an interactive video. In any case, most new hires get little more than a brief introduction to company values before they are expected to demonstrate them on the job.

By contrast, the Marines' entire recruiting and training period is devoted to ensuring that new recruits comprehend the institution's core values of honor, courage, and commitment. The first time a potential recruit encounters the Corps' values is during his "cultivation interview" on a high school campus or in a Marines storefront. While most companies use headhunters and human resources people to ferret out potential workers, the Marines assign the job to the best of their experienced sergeants and midcareer officers, individuals having what can only be described as a missionary zeal about the Marines' values. Such fervor is an important screening device. Individuals who come back for a second interview have taken a step toward accepting the values of the MVP path.

At boot camp, the emphasis on values intensifies, as our research team discovered firsthand. The Marines treated our visiting group like new recruits when we arrived on Parris Island, ordering us off the bus and instructing us to place our feet precisely onto yellow footprints painted on the pavement. Our team leader, McKinsey principal Brad Berkson, who has never served in the military, quickly found himself barking "Yes, sir!" and "No, sir!" to the shouted questions of the drill instructor. We were led into a small room, where a sergeant delivered a speech on the importance of integrity. Following that stern but impassioned speech, would-be Marines are handed their official records—completed during the recruiting process—and asked to check them for accuracy. Have they honestly described any history of substance abuse? Have they reported every run-in with the law? The recruits are told, "If you did it, we will find it. So don't start your career here with a lie." Over the next hour or more, recruits file to the front of the room and come clean, showing they are ready to embrace the values of honor, courage, and commitment—perhaps for the first time in their lives.

Unlike other branches of the armed forces, the Marines do not promise technical training in fields such as electronics or aviation. Instead, days are filled with physically and emotionally stressful exercises designed to encourage mutual accountability. If a recruit fails to complete a 15-mile endurance hike, his comrades must carry his rifle and 60-pound rucksack for the rest of the

hike. If someone errs during a close-order-drill movement, the entire unit must repeat the movement until it
is flawless. In every training event, strong performers are
expected to help their less proficient comrades.

As with its recruiters, the Corps assigns its very best
to be boot-camp drill instructors. Only the top 25% of
enlisted noncommissioned officers are even considered
for DI assignment. Of that group, only 80% make it
through the rigorous Drill Instructors School. The
assignment is seen as an honor and a career enhance-
ment: given the relative scarcity of promotions in the
post-Cold War era, a three-year tour as a DI often determines whether an enlisted Marine's career will reach 20
years. The result is that the screening, selection, training,
and shaping of those on the front line rests in the hands
of the highest-performing leaders.

Through the intense focus on values, Marine recruit-
ment and training build a sense of belonging to a noble
cause. Indeed, training culminates in a 54-hour continuous field exercise called the Crucible, in which recruits
struggle through a series of grueling challenges—including combat assaults through mud pits and under
machine-gun fire—with little sleep or food. Throughout
the ordeal, trainers constantly cite the heroic acts of
Medal of Honor winners, thereby personalizing each
recruit's concept of what it means to be a Marine. That
identification with the organization—the recruits' pride
in the Corps, in themselves, and in their units—sustains
a high level of energy and loyalty to the organization for
a long time after Marines leave boot camp.

While the Marine Corps' investment in inculcating
values may seem extreme to outsiders, its practices can
be translated for the business context. For some companies, emulating the Marines on this front might

require only a shift of emphasis during initial training. Instead of covering values as an add-on topic at the end of orientation, trainers within business could bring them to center stage early on. At Marriott, for example, a week-long examination of company values culminates with new employees role playing in realistic scenarios that require them to apply the company's values when making tough decisions.

A company need not have a Guadalcanal in its past to celebrate itself. The victories of the business battlefield are plenty to draw upon.

Businesses also might assign training to their most experienced and talented managers and increase the length of training programs from a matter of hours to days or even weeks. Those steps will carry costs, of course. But think of them as investments that will have large dividends. One outstanding role model might influence 40 or 50 new hires, whose commitment and focus could save the company millions of dollars in the long run.

Finally, to bolster collective pride in their frontline employees, companies can continue to focus on values after training ends. Southwest Airlines posts hundreds of documents and photos highlighting the company's accomplishments in the lobby of its headquarters building. Marriott prominently displays letters from customers praising superior service. A company need not have a Guadalcanal in its past to celebrate itself. The victories of the business battlefield are plenty to draw upon.

Practice Two: Prepare every person to lead, including frontline supervisors. Most businesses separate their frontline employees into two camps: followers and potential leaders. The followers are written off or given superficial attention; they receive no training to develop their abilities. The group of potential leaders is usually small, because most companies use the standard business-leadership template to identify individuals who might move up. The template includes a slim list of predictable attributes—thinks strategically, delegates, sets and meets demanding targets—even though most executives know from experience that effective leadership styles are many and varied.

The Marines don't distinguish between followers and potential leaders; they believe every member of the Corps must be able to lead. Consider the exigencies of battle. The 19-year-old lance corporal who suddenly finds himself facing an angry mob on the streets of Haiti must know when and how to use force. Indeed, the nature of war dictates that Marines must be trained to do more than just take orders. In a flash of gunfire, any Marine may find that he's the person responsible for giving orders. That is why every enlisted Marine learns how to run a fire team—the basic four-person unit of Marine operations—and every officer learns how to run a 40-member rifle platoon.

The policy of training every frontline person to lead has a powerful impact on morale. The organization's belief that everyone can and must be a leader creates enormous collective pride and builds mutual trust. Each Marine knows he can rely on his comrades to take charge, just as he can be relied on. With the two building blocks of the MVP path—pride and trust—firmly in place, energy and commitment naturally follow.

Enlisted Marines are introduced to the fundamentals of leadership at boot camp, where drill instructors serve as 24-hour-a-day role models. The instructors' goal at this stage is not to teach young recruits how to take charge but to demonstrate the qualities that characterize effective leaders in action: morality, courage, initiative, and respect for others. Drill instructors embody the highest standards of Marine behavior. They rise at 4:30 AM, at least a half-hour before the recruits in their command; during endurance hikes, when recruits are allowed to sit for a ten-minute break, they remain standing with their heavy packs on; and their appearance is at all times flawless, as is their composure.

For college graduates who join the Marines, formal leadership training begins almost right away at Officer Candidates School in Quantico, Virginia. Marines who will soon lead platoons—basically as frontline supervisors—spend ten weeks learning the practical and theoretical components of running an organization, from logistics to motivation. This stands in stark contrast to the standard operating procedure in business, where the vast majority of newly minted supervisors receive limited, cookie-cutter instruction in what it means to be a leader. The Marines believe that the energy of those in the front lines is largely driven by the energy of frontline supervisors, so they make leadership development a priority.

To that end, OCS trainers seek to identify and hone each officer's unique approach to leadership. Contrary to the stereotype of the inflexible command-and-control style, the Marine Corps recognizes and cultivates several styles of effective leadership, such as assertive, collaborative, insightful, and supportive. To determine which approach best fits each individual, trainers put officer candidates through a series of exercises that simulate battlefield conditions. For instance, candidates in groups of four or five must decide how to rescue a wounded

Marine (a 250-pound dummy) from the far side of a moat, beyond a mock-up of a burned-out bridge, without getting wet or touching certain off-limits areas. The team has no designated leader and nothing to work with except three five-foot boards. The problem is technically solvable (though rarely in the time allowed), but the instructors are mostly interested in the leadership capabilities and shortfalls each member demonstrates.

As the students' leadership capabilities begin to emerge, the candidates are counseled and advised by experienced observers, usually captains. These observers, who spend up to 16 hours a day with the officer candidates, are trained to look for various leadership attributes, advise the students of their strengths and weaknesses, and coach them on how to make the most of their leadership potential. The process is anything but standardized.

The Marine Corps also develops leadership skills among its frontline supervisors by routinely establishing what we call "leadership partnerships" in the Fleet Marine Force. Each platoon is run by two individuals: the higher-ranking officer, a young lieutenant with one to three years' experience, is paired with a seasoned staff sergeant or gunnery sergeant with 12 to 18 years' experience. The experience and maturity of the sergeant complement the tactical education and fresh ideas of the lieutenant. The two learn from each other and jointly solve tactical challenges and problems about people. The learning is stimulating and energizing for both, as well as for those in their command. Each leader has more time to attend to

To emulate the Marines, executives would need to embrace the idea that many frontline workers can lead.

the training and professional growth of the platoon's 40 or more members than if he were the sole officer in charge. That kind of personal attention is another force for building the energy and commitment of the rank and file. (For a firsthand account of such a partnership, see "Learning While Leading" at the end of this article.)

Most business executives would see a leadership partnership as wasteful, but the positive effects of the combination—in terms of performance—usually make up for any additional costs. Moreover, the arrangement accelerates the development of younger leaders, which adds to the leadership capacity and performance capabilities of the enterprise as a whole. Such intangibles may well prove priceless in the long term.

To emulate the Corps' leadership development initiative, business executives would first need to shake off their old attitudes. They would need to embrace the notion that a great many frontline workers can lead and thus should be trained to do so. Executives would need to support the idea that every frontline supervisor deserves extensive leadership training with an approach that makes the most of the supervisor's individual leadership style. These are major attitude adjustments— probably more than most businesspeople are willing to accept all at once. Too often, managers assume that "leadership" is an intrinsic quality that somehow emerges on its own. That's why training frontline leaders is frequently left to mentors. Changing this approach is far from easy, and like many humbling attitude adjustments in life, the payoff is best appreciated in hindsight.

A less jarring way for executives to introduce this change is to create informal leadership partnerships. Newly appointed managers could be assigned, ad hoc, to work with more experienced veterans in the running of a division or a department. This might mean that both members of the duo would do less managing and more hands-on work, but it would expand capabilities, and in time would change minds about leadership development.

Practice Three: Distinguish between teams and single-leader work groups. One of the most common—and damaging—occurrences in business is executives putting together single-leader work groups and calling them teams. Usually the practice is unintentional; most executives don't know the difference between the two arrangements. But such a mistake confuses and demotivates people and undermines the performance of small groups. Take the case of the CEO of an energy company that was midway through a major turnaround. The CEO thought of his five direct reports as a team and often encouraged them to join him in mapping out new strategies for the company. But the truth is that he was using the executives only to bolster his preconceived views. On key issues, he invariably resorted to one-on-one discussions and then made decisions that his "team" approved but did not jointly influence. The five executives saw through the situation and soon grew frustrated and resentful, while the CEO remained convinced that he was nourishing a cohesive team. Calling a group a team doesn't make it one.

Real teams are rare. Most work in business is done by single-leader work groups, which rely entirely on their leaders for purpose, goals, motivation, and assignments; each member is accountable solely to the leader. Single-leader work groups have an important place in organizational life. They are fast and efficient, and they can be a great help when individual tasks are more important than collective work and when the leader really does know best how to get things done.

A real team, by contrast, draws its motivation more from its mission and goals than from its leader. Members work together as peers and hold one another accountable for the group's performance and results. In a real team, no individual member can win or lose; only the group can succeed or fail.

Given the amount of ink devoted to extolling teams in the past decade, many executives are loath to put people together in anything but. That's why the cleaning employees and their supervisor at your hotel are a "customer service team," and the clerks and store manager at your supermarket are a "check-out efficiency team." These are really single-leader work groups, or, worse, they are single-leader work groups in which flagging morale and participation on the part of the group have caused the leader to back off from the supervisory role. The result of these "compromise units" is typically anger and inertia. Trust and confidence are bolstered when people know what is expected of them and their colleagues. And when goals and responsibilities are clear, they can be exceeded—another energy booster.

The Marines are masters at distinguishing between single-leader work groups and teams, partly because the Corps maintains a culture of extreme clarity—you can't be vague about battle directives. Another reason is that the Marines explicitly teach people the differences between roles. At infantry school, after boot camp, each Marine rotates through all the positions in a fire team—leader, machine-gunner, assistant machine-gunner, and rifleman—and learns when and how to shift the leadership role. By the time the team is ready for active duty, each member can fill every position. Most important, the highly cohesive group has learned when and how to function as a real team and when to rely on a single leader.

For businesses to adopt the practice of distinguishing between teams and single-leader work groups, executives would first need to understand the differences between the two. (For a summary of these distinctions, see the exhibit "Teams and Work Groups: It Pays to Know the Difference.") Furthermore, executives would need to bring this knowledge to bear in managing the front line. That requires discipline on the part of the executives. People generally like to be assigned to teams; they are less enamored of being assigned to something called a "single-leader work group." But in the long run, clarity creates trust.

Practice Four: Attend to the bottom half. Businesses, in general, are relentless about leveraging their leaders' time. That's why frontline managers are usually trained to focus their attention on the people who have the greatest potential to advance. An assumption is built into most evaluation systems that people in the lower half will function adequately or leave.

The Marines do not have that luxury, because the graduates of boot camp cannot be replaced for four years unless they violate the Uniform Code of Military Justice with serious offenses such as stealing or drug use. Moreover, a Marine unit in battle is only as strong as its weakest link. A poor performer puts lives in danger. The Marines simply cannot afford to let the bottom half languish.

Like executives in the corporate world, leaders in the Marine Corps have little time to spare, but they find the time to attend to poor and mediocre performers, even if it means personal sacrifice. Consider the case of Colonel Al Davis, who made it a point to get to know every member of each class of 300 officer candidates while serving

Teams and Work Groups: It Pays to Know the Difference

Managers tend to label every working group in an organization a "team," whether it's a roomful of customer service operators or a string of assemblers on a manufacturing line. But employees quickly lose motivation and commitment when they're assigned to a team that turns out to be a single-leader work group. If executives want to spark energy and commitment on the front lines, they must know how a team differs from a single-leader work group, and when to create one or the other.

	Team	Single-Leader Work Group
Run by:	the members of the team best-suited to lead the tasks at hand; the leadership role shifts among the members	one person, usually the senior member, who is formally designated to lead
Goals and agenda set by:	the group, based on dialogue about purpose; constructive conflict and integration predominate	the formal leader, often in consultation with a sponsoring executive; conflict with group members is avoided, and the leader integrates
Performance evaluated by:	the members of the group, as well as the leader and sponsor	the leader and the sponsor
Work style determined by:	the members	the leader's preference
Success defined by:	the members' aspirations	the leader's aspirations
Most appropriate business context:	a complex challenge that requires people with various skill sets working together much of the time	a challenge in which time is of the essence and the leader already knows best how to proceed; the leader is the primary integrator
Speed and efficiency:	low until the group has learned to function as a team; afterward, however, the team is as fast as a single-leader group	higher than that of teams initially, as the members need no time to develop commitment or to learn to work as a team
Primary end-products:	largely collective, requiring several team members to work together to produce results	largely individual and can be accomplished best by each person working on his or her own
Accountability characterized by:	"We hold one another mutually accountable for achieving the goals and performance of the team."	"The leader holds us individually accountable for our output."

as commanding officer of OCS from 1995 to 1997. Colonel Davis regularly participated in physical exercises with the officer candidates, and whenever a student came up for "disenrollment review," he made it his goal to find a way to help rather than dismiss. Colonel Davis personally made every final decision to expel or reassign, based on a thorough discussion involving all the officers who had worked with each student.

Colonel Davis's commitment to every last Marine is not unique. Drill instructors, despite their legendary toughness, refuse to give up on any recruit. Incoming Marines are told, "You may give up on yourself more than once during the next 12 weeks, but we will never give up on you." In one interview with a member of the research team, a drill instructor said he and his colleagues see each new recruit as a psychological puzzle to be solved. He noted, "We use every tool we can—whatever works."

The impact of this principle is powerful. Personal attention means that floundering Marines are caught before they hit bottom. That approach reinforces the individual's sense of belonging and builds an intense loyalty to the organization. Loyalty and a sense of belonging are components of the mutual trust that is critical to the MVP path. The Marines' approach also prevents any individual from feeling that he's bound to fail. The effect is more pride, both personal and collective.

Most business managers resist devoting time and talent to the bottom half. They believe it's easier and cheaper to replace any underperformers than to rejuvenate them. Perhaps that was once true, but in places where the economy is booming, labor is in short supply. Many companies that once seemed to have an unlimited number of applicants for low-level positions are now struggling to keep every job filled. For that reason alone, salvaging underperformers makes sense. Then add the positive energy the practice engenders, and the Marines' approach seems purely logical.

Devoting more time and attention to the bottom half does not necessarily have to cost a lot. Sometimes all it requires is creative hiring of frontline supervisors— recruiting people with experience in counseling or teaching, for instance. Some insurance companies, notably State Farm, have been successful in hiring former high school teachers as supervising agents, and A. L. Williams, now Primerica Financial Services, has hired former high school football coaches. These agents have skills in teaching and firsthand knowledge of how to keep talented but undisciplined young people on track. As an alternative to hiring experienced teachers, companies can train supervisors to work with the bottom half. Many companies already teach managers team-building and communication skills. There is no reason not to expand that repertoire.

Companies also might invest in training and development programs focused on employees who are at risk of falling through the cracks. Marriott has a six-week program specifically designed for frontline workers who are former welfare recipients or who were hired from the ranks of the homeless. Launched in 1991, the Pathways to Independence program offers instruction in life skills, such as opening a bank account and using public transportation, in addition to work skills, such as cleaning a hotel room efficiently. Pathways instructors also advise participants on work etiquette—why it is important to show up on time and be well groomed (teachers suggest, for instance, that participants trim facial hair and shed most jewelry). The training pays off in retention rates. In the Washington, D.C., area, the percentage of new employees remaining on the job longer than one year was higher among Pathways graduates than among comparable workers who hadn't had training—75% versus less than 65%.

Companies also can increase the likelihood that frontline supervisors will attend to underperformers simply by evaluating the supervisors on that dimension of their jobs. GE does this by routinely surveying frontline employees on job satisfaction and holding supervisors accountable for the results. Because underperformers are typically unhappy at work, such surveys essentially prevent managers from writing them off. At GE, it is well known that "the numbers no longer protect," that managers cannot achieve their financial goals at the expense of their people.

Practice Five: Use discipline to build pride. Many organizations regard discipline as a necessary evil: a tool to keep order, but the enemy of empowerment. Discipline is seen as a top-down method of control and punishment. Supervisors fire people who are habitually late or dock the pay of workers who violate the dress code. No one expects such measures to engender energy or build commitment.

The Marines respect discipline as control and punishment, but they also see it as an opportunity to build pride. The Marines have rules, and plenty of them. You obey those rules or you're out. But the Marines put equal emphasis on self-discipline and group-discipline. They ask every member of the front line to be his own toughest boss and to be a strict enforcer for his comrades. Such a dynamic could backfire in other circumstances— for instance, if the underlying values of the institution were corrupt. But in their approach to discipline, the Marines are demanding that everyone on the front line act with honor, courage, and commitment. When people do so—on their own and as a group—enormous energy is unleashed.

The fact is, many Marine recruits begin their careers with a vast repertoire of sloppy behaviors that include foul language, poor work habits, and disrespectful treatment of others. In that sense, they are not unlike the people many companies try (unsuccessfully) to screen out. And so the first few miles of a recruit's journey toward greater discipline look and sound a lot like what happens in business—lots of harsh repercussions for breaking the rules.

Within the first month, however, the relentless crush of discipline is well on its way to molding a positive self-image in most recruits. They discover what they are capable of when they apply themselves. Then they discover that they can accomplish more than they ever thought possible. Next they learn that group-discipline means nobody will be left behind in battle. Before boot camp is over, recruits come to see that discipline does not exist just for discipline's sake; it ensures a widespread commitment to mission, values, and comrades.

Like the Marines, every MVP company studied by our research team encourages self-discipline in order to build pride. The results are remarkable. Southwest Airlines turns its planes around in less than half the time needed by many of its competitors. The main reasons are employee self-discipline and the group-discipline practiced by its work groups. Employees

It takes very little to get frontline employees to set and beat their own standards for performance.

undertake their tasks with fervor, not out of fear of punishment, but out of a desire to make their airline the best. It is common to see baggage handlers, flight attendants, and pilots scrambling to beat the clock and encouraging others to do the same. Sometimes crew members actually help baggage handlers, and vice versa—something unheard of at other airlines.

Similarly, Marriott's housekeepers drive themselves—and one another—to get rooms clean in less than 24 minutes; bellmen hustle to get guests checked in and to their rooms with no delays or complaints. These behaviors are strongly encouraged by Marriott executives. But to talk to these employees is to know that they are driven by self-discipline and group-discipline—an ardent desire to follow the rules in order to make themselves and the organization proud.

It takes very little to harness the positive power of discipline, to get frontline employees to set and beat their own high standards for performance. It starts with an executive decision never to be content with enterprise-imposed, top-down discipline, and a commitment to encouraging self-discipline and group-discipline. One simple method is to call attention to workers who demonstrate self-discipline: feature them in a company newsletter, honor them with conspicuous awards. Such actions build pride and serve as an invaluable example for others.

Another powerful means to induce self-discipline and peer-enforced discipline is to display shortfalls, particularly those that are apparent to customers. The self-discipline and peer-enforced discipline we observed at Marriott were due in no small measure to the company's practice of posting all guest complaints for employees to see.

From the Battlefield to the Boardroom

No executive of an organization that depends on its rank and file can afford to ignore the example set by the Marines. A skeptic might argue that the Marines have an incomparable advantage: a long history of a fired-up front line. Their emotional energy is genetic, so to speak. But the Marines have had setbacks along the way. The Vietnam War deeply eroded the Corps' values and esprit. Indeed, it nearly broke them. The great tragedy of the 1983 terrorist bombing of a Marine barracks in Beirut, which killed 241 Marines, sailors, and soldiers, also took an enormous toll on the Corps' emotional energy. The Marines had to rebuild their shared values and collective pride nearly from scratch. They were as new to the MVP path as any start-up.

But what is perhaps most persuasive about the Marines' approach to energizing the front lines is that the five underlying managerial practices can be found in nonmilitary organizations today. Rarely, however, are those practices pursued with the dedication, rigor, and relentless determination necessary to convert ordinary workers into an extraordinary work force. The Corps does that, and the corporation can, too.

Learning While Leading

IN 1997, I WAS appointed the commanding officer of a frontline combat unit that comprised 125 Marines. The assignment, normally reserved for a senior captain, carried tremendous responsibility for a 26-year-old lieutenant with just two years of active duty. Fortunately, I was paired with First Sergeant Ian V. Smith, an enlisted professional and combat veteran with 22 years of experience. I learned more about leadership from First Sergeant Smith during the four months we worked together than I had from any other Marine, officer or enlisted, in the previous two years.

The learning process began the day after our partnership was formed. My overly ambitious plan to issue gas masks and have the Marines clean weapons in the same afternoon caused the members of the group to miss dinner. Morale suffered. The next day, First Sergeant Smith offered me his frank assessment of what went wrong, beginning with the words, "Sir, your plan failed because you did not consult the experienced leaders of this unit. We have conducted this drill countless times before." From then on, I relied heavily on his advice.

First Sergeant Smith also taught me the importance of developing others. He often placed his busy schedule on hold to teach young enlisted Marines about the Corps' history and traditions as well as its leadership principles and values. The dividends of his efforts were almost immediately apparent: his students soon began to exercise greater initiative and assume more responsibility for daily tasks.

Finally, First Sergeant Smith taught me a lesson I will always carry with me: that leaders inspire people by demonstrating a genuine concern for their welfare. Whenever a Marine faced a personal emergency, First Sergeant Smith focused his undivided attention on the problem until it was resolved. If Marines were temporarily transferred to other units, he periodically visited them to ensure that their needs were being met. Every time one of the Marines completed technical school or a leadership course, he attended the graduation ceremony and shared in the accomplishment. His efforts built an intense loyalty to the unit and inspired every one of its members to achieve higher levels of performance.

I have not yet been afforded the leadership responsibility in the business world that I had in the Marine Corps. But I know that when the time comes to run a team or even an organization, I will be guided by the insights gained in my short but immensely powerful partnership with First Sergeant Smith.

Jason A. Santamaria

Originally published in May–June 1999
Reprint 99307

Preventing the Premature Death of Relationship Marketing

SUSAN FOURNIER, SUSAN DOBSCHA, AND
DAVID GLEN MICK

Executive Summary

RELATIONSHIP MARKETING is in vogue. And why not? The new, increasingly efficient ways that companies have of understanding and responding to customers' needs and preferences seemingly allow them to build more meaningful connections with consumers than ever before. These connections promise to benefit the bottom line by reducing costs and increasing revenue.

Unfortunately, a close look suggests that the relationships between companies and customers are troubled ones, at best. Companies may delight in learning more about their customers and in being able to provide features and services to please every possible palate. But customers delight in neither. In fact, customer satisfaction rates in the United States are at an all-time low, while complaints, boycotts, and other expressions of consumer discontent are on the rise. This mounting wave of unhappiness has yet to reach the bottom line. Sooner or later, however, corporate performance will suffer unless relationship marketing becomes what it is supposed to be—the epitome of customer orientation.

Ironically, the very things that marketers are doing to build relationships with customers are often the things that are destroying those relationships. Relationship marketing is powerful in theory but troubled in practice. To prevent its premature death, marketers need to take the time to figure out how and why they are undermining their own best efforts, as well as how they can get things back on track.

RELATIONSHIP MARKETING is in vogue. Managers talk it up. Companies profess to do it in new and better ways every day. Academics extol its merits. And why not? The new, increasingly efficient ways that companies have of understanding and responding to customers' needs and preferences seemingly allow them to build more meaningful connections with consumers than ever before. These connections promise to benefit the bottom line by reducing costs and increasing revenues.

Unfortunately, a close look suggests that relationships between companies and consumers are troubled at best. When we talk to people about their lives as consumers, we do not hear praise for their so-called corporate partners. Instead, we hear about the confusing, stressful, insensitive, and manipulative marketplace in which they feel trapped and victimized. Companies may delight in learning more about their customers than ever before and in providing features and services to please every possible palate. But customers delight in neither. Customers cope. They tolerate sales clerks who hound them with questions every time they buy a battery. They muddle through the plethora of products that line grocery store shelves. They deal with the glut of new features in their computers and cameras. They juggle the flood of invitations to participate in frequent-buyer rewards programs. Customer satisfaction rates in the United States are at an all-time low, while complaints, boycotts, and other expressions of consumer discontent rise. This mounting wave of unhappiness has yet to reach the bottom line. Sooner or later, however, corporate performance will suffer unless relationship marketing becomes what it is supposed to be: the epitome of customer orientation.

Ironically, the very things that marketers are doing to build relationships with customers are often the things that are destroying those relationships. Why? Perhaps we are skimming over the fundamentals of relationship building in our rush to cash in on the potential rewards of creating close connections with our customers. Perhaps we do not understand what creating a relationship really means; that is, how customers' trust and intimacy factor into the connections we are trying to forge. Relationship marketing is powerful in theory but troubled in practice. To prevent its premature death, we need to take the time to figure out how and why we are undermining our own best efforts, as well as how we can get things back on track.

Seeing Through the Eyes of the Consumer

Caught up in our enthusiasm for our information-gathering capabilities and for the potential opportunities that long-term engagements with customers hold, is it possible that we have forgotten that relationships take two? Is it possible that we haven't looked close enough to see that the consumer is not necessarily a willing participant in our relationship mission? Consider relationship marketing from the consumer's point of view.

The number of one-on-one relationships that companies ask consumers to maintain is untenable. As a result, many marketing initiatives seem trivial and useless instead of unique and valuable. Every company wants the rewards of long-term, committed partnerships. But people maintain literally hundreds of one-on-one relationships in their personal lives—with spouses, co-workers, casual acquaintances. And clearly, only a handful of them are of a close and committed nature. How can we expect people to do anymore in their lives as consumers?

"It's overkill," said one woman we interviewed, referring to the number of advances she fields from companies wanting to initiate or improve their relationship with her. "One is more meaningless than the next. I must get ten mailings every day. When I go away for vacation, the accumulation is remarkable. I never look inside the mailings anymore. I just throw them all away."

"The flood of advances from companies undermines any one overture so that it doesn't matter which company you end up doing business with," said another disillusioned customer. "I started with phone company A, then switched to company B. I got some reward from the second company for switching—I don't remember what. Then company A paid me to come back. It was like I was hunted prey—$50 here, $50 there, $100 to leave company A a second time. I was a college student at the time, and the money was great. But it was crazy. The salespeople on both sides kept telling me how important a customer

I was to them, but who pays you to be their customer? I wasn't developing a relationship with either company. I was just taking the money."

There's a balance between giving and getting in a good relationship. But when companies ask their customers for friendship, loyalty, and respect, too often they don't give those customers friendship, loyalty, and respect in return. How do we follow through on the assertion that we value one-on-one relationships with our customers? One woman told us of her frustration at being asked to disclose personal information each time she patronizes a certain hotel chain. "I volunteer vital statistics every time," she explained. "Name, address, method of payment, travel for business or pleasure, number of hotel visits per year. The use to which this information is put remains a mystery to me. Do the clerks know who uses the information and how? No. Are product offerings improved? Not to my knowledge. Do I get a special discount? Certainly not. Am I greeted in some special way each time I return? No. And for that matter, suppose I was? If a company did 'remember' what drink I ordered from room service the last time I stayed in the hotel, who's to say that I'd want it again? I don't always order a diet soft drink."

Do marketers understand how customers' trust and intimacy factor into the connections they are trying to forge?

The disconnect between the "give" and the "get" was particularly revealing in one consumer's story of his interactions with a catalog company. "The company has what seems to be a good idea," he recounted. "Each year around the holidays, it sends out a reminder to its customers, telling them what they ordered the year before and for whom. The problem is, several years ago I ordered presents for the physicians who took care of my mother when she was hospitalized for an emergency medical condition. And each year now, the company reminds me of that awful time. I even called the company and explained that I don't generally buy presents for the people on that list. I told them why, and I asked for those names to be deleted. The operator was nice enough on the phone and said that the names would be taken off my list. But this fall, there they were again."

The net effect, according to another consumer we talked to, is relationship marketing that is all "one way": "Sure, they can call me at dinner, but I can't reach them on the phone. They can send me 100 pieces of mail per year, but I can't register one meaningful response with them. You really want to be my friend? Sure you do. Well, then, what are you going to do for me? Or more to the point, how much is it going to cost me? Companies claim that they're interested in the customer. But the focus is not on the customer—it's on the company."

Companies' claims that customer relationships are valued don't hold water. Sometimes people feel put at a disadvantage by their loyalty. And sometimes a company's preoccupation with its so-called best customers leaves other revenue-generating customers feeling left out and underappreciated. New customers at certain credit-card companies get special introductory interest rates while fees for long-standing customers skyrocket. Loyal customers are inundated with inappropriate or seemingly insignificant corporate mailings—mailings that sometimes treat them as brand-new marketing targets, ignoring their long-standing tenure. One savvy consumer summed up the phenomenon: "Are these the rewards or the punishments of relationship marketing?"

And what of those loyal customers who don't happen to spend enough money to get into a company's inner circle? "I rent cars from one particular company," said one man. "You could call me a loyal customer. I never rent from any other company. But as I learned on my last trip, I am apparently not one of the company's valued customers. We were taking the van from the airport to the rental lot, and the driver asks, 'Who here is a club member?' Three people raise their hands and, one by one, get dropped off at their cars. They get all this special treatment, and the rest of us are just sitting there looking around at one another, feeling uncomfortable. Finally, one guy looks at me and says, 'What makes them so special?' I started to explain that those are the company's big-ticket customers, that they spend a lot of money with the company. But as I was talking, I was thinking, Hell, I spend a lot of money here, too. I should be a valued customer. But instead, the company is making me feel like chopped liver. It made me really mad."

In their role as relationship partners, companies need people to think of them as allies and friends; but more often than not, they come across as enemies. Companies claim to offer solutions to consumers' problems; but in fact, they are creating more problems than they solve. Supermarket SKUs have risen to 32,000, with more than 2,500 new products on the shelf vying for attention. Coke is available in more than 50 product and packaging variations, Crest in 55. Snapple at one time logged more than 70 flavor varieties on grocers' shelves—despite the fact that 6 flavors commanded the majority of the company's sales. Some cable television systems on the market today offer more than 700 different channels, though research has shown that the average user is happy to handle 10.

Companies are trying to satisfy—and log a sale on—
customers' every desire or fleeting whim. But customers
view the scene differently. They see a bewildering array
of seemingly undifferentiated product offerings. Companies tend to center their efforts on the potential advantages of being first to market with new, technologically
superior products. They view negative feedback from
consumers as merely temporary resistance to change. An
alternative explanation begs notice, however: optimal
levels of choice exist, and current product policies consistently exceed those marks.

"I nearly cried the last time I went to buy something
for my headache," one woman said. "Did I have a tension,
sinus, or recurring headache? Did I want aspirin, ibupro-
fen, acetaminophen? Store brand or major brand? I don't
know all the answers, but I do know that my headache
got worse thinking about them. I just stood there looking
at the shelf. I was paralyzed."

"I tried to do something about the chaos," another
disgruntled customer recounted. "I was being deluged by
catalogs—three, four, five a day. I was saturated with
options. I had to put a stop to it. So I called one company
that I actually like. I asked
where the company had
gotten my name. After a
few calls, I finally got
someone who could tell
me. It was another com-
pany. So I called that company. And so on, and so
on. With every call, I regis-
tered my deep disappointment that the company would
sell my name and my purchase preferences without my
permission. No one seemed to care. The best any of them

*Loss of control,
vulnerability, stress:
these themes emerge
when consumers talk about
products, companies,
even the marketplace as
a whole.*

could do was to agree to take my name off their list—a change that most said wouldn't take effect for about six months. Finally, I gave up. New catalogs kept coming in. I was defeated."

Loss of control, vulnerability, stress, victimization: these are the themes that emerge when we listen to people talk about the products they use, the companies that supply them, and the marketplace as a whole. In fact, we are more likely to hear consumers vent their frustrations about newly acquired products than we are to hear them extol their virtues. Control is experienced simultaneously as loss of control. Gains in efficiency are offset by the creation of more work. Freedom of choice is interpreted as a bind of commitments. These frustrations run deep, threatening the very quality of consumers' lives.

As one consumer said, "The answering machine is great. I catch all these calls that I would have missed otherwise. I don't have to be home to receive calls. But at the same time, I become a slave to that technology. The machine makes me come home and check it every day. The first things I do when I get home: check the mailbox, check the answering machine. And then you are responsible for returning all those calls. If you had no machine, who would be the wiser? It's like a plant. You have to water it to keep it alive."

Consumers view companies as enemies, not allies. They don't welcome our advances. They arm themselves to fight back.

"We got a weed eater, and what I have found in having that thing is that you tend not to be quite as conscious about what you are going to trim," said another consumer. "My wife planted little flower beds here and there, and around trees, and it was like, 'No, problem. We have the weed eater!' The problem here isn't that you bought a product and it didn't do its job. The problem is that because the product made something easier, you ended up working more than you would have before. The weed eater led to more weeding! Most technological products do their jobs, and do them well, but they end up generating more work."

The net effect is a consumer who is more likely to view companies as enemies, not allies. Our research suggests that consumers develop coping strategies designed to eliminate, minimize, or otherwise control the deleterious effects the marketplace has on the quality of their lives. Consumers develop "purchase and consumption rules" to get them through the day. They may refuse to set the clock on their VCRs, for example, or they may put off purchasing an item to avoid the challenges of owning it. They also may constrain the use of certain products to limit the negative effects those products have on their lives, say, by leaving their portable phones behind when they work in the garden. They may even hire a professional organizer to help them sift through the chaos and downsize their choices to manageable levels. Consumers don't welcome our advances. They arm themselves to fight back.

Regaining Trust

In 1985, psychologists Michael Argyle and Monica Henderson, professors at Oxford University, defined several basic universal rules of friendship. Among them: provide emotional support, respect privacy and preserve confidences, and be tolerant of other friendships. We've violated each of these rules. In so doing, we've forfeited our customers' trust and, with it, the chance to build the intimacy that results in truly rewarding partnerships. How can we regain that trust? We must start to behave in ways that will show consumers that companies can be valued partners. We have to prove through our actions that marketing relationships need not be empty, meaningless, or stressful at best.

Judging from consumers' tales, the best place to start is with our new-product-development policies and projects. Time-to-market imperatives, for instance, should be reconsidered from the consumer's point of view. According to marketing researcher Jonlee Andrews, the key reason companies launch extensions that customers perceive as meaningless is that, from inside a rigid brand-management organizational structure, managers simply can't tell what will resonate with consumers and what won't. We need to break out of that mold, recognize that endless introductions create noise not need, and be more rigorous about evaluating consumers' likely reactions to our new products and extensions.

For example, in the area of product design, we might do well to engage social scientists. Their expertise would help engineers eliminate the kinds of features and functions that frustrate or overwhelm consumers. Sony regularly engages cultural anthropologists for this task, whereas Sharp prefers sociologists. Both practices make salient the "human" side of design—where concerns about product performance are augmented by aesthetics and a genuine effort to improve the quality of people's daily lives. Similarly, we could try harder to ensure that our existing product lines adhere to a quality-of-life-based mission. Some companies seem to be addressing that issue. Procter & Gamble has standardized its products' formulas and packages, reduced its deluge of promotions and coupons, pruned marginal brands from its lines, and cut back on its dizzying array of new-product launches. Computer manufacturers are offering more user-friendly features and enhanced service support. Auto manufacturers have trimmed product lines on many models and brands by offering platform-based value packages. Some thoughtful initiatives offer customers tangible tools to control the frustrations that overwhelm them. America Online has designed software enhancements that allow customers to block unsolicited E-mail messages; many major department stores now offer "purchase pals" to help customers sort through the dizzying array of products; and a Microsoft-led initiative, called the Simply Interactive PC, promises to make it easier for users to upgrade their machines, quelling the fears of premature obsolescence that plague leading edge buyers.

But we must ask ourselves, Are these initiatives, and others like them, undertaken with a genuine concern for consumers' emotional well-being? In positioning for simplicity, are we solving the problem or taking advantage of it? When consumers have to pay a fee for telephone-software-support service after only 90 days of owning their computers, has the fundamental problem been solved? When consumers pay extra each month for the privilege of overriding their caller-identification feature, have we addressed the basic issue? Are SKUs being cut for the consumer's sake, or is an empathetic stance just a good way to spin cost cutting?

Once we have our product policies in line, we must rethink the way we solicit and handle our customers' personal information. The information that companies need to build lasting long-term relationships is extremely private and valuable, so we must treat it with care. We need to remember a forgotten rule: that intimacy and vulnerability are entwined. For example, if a company routinely asks its customers for sensitive information but doesn't put that information to use, it should stop asking those questions. We must force ourselves out of that safe place where information may someday prove useful for an as-yet-to-be-articulated question and recognize the cumulative price of eroded consumer confidence along the way. We pay for those invasions, so let's make sure the cost is worth it.

Finally, we must begin to confront our own relationship goals honestly. We can't expect to develop intense, devoted relationships with every consumer of every product or brand we offer. Why pretend that we can? Let's put our relationship motives on the table: no fluff, no faked sincerity, no obtuse language, no promises we don't keep—just honesty about commercial intent. We want consumers' money—let's tell them that, and let's tell them why the deal's a good one. Nielsen

For contemporary consumers, **product** *satisfaction is linked to* life *satisfaction, and companies must attend to both to win.*

Media Research has recently converted its panelists into "members" who have the "privilege of volunteering to be Nielsen households." Do those families feel any different now than they did before? Are the company's panelists allied to the company in a more meaningful way than they were in the past? Or has the language fallen flat because there's nothing to support it?

Attaining Intimacy

Even if we approach all of the above directives with the same zeal with which we have embraced the call of relationship marketing, we still face a tough hurdle. True customer intimacy—the backbone of a successful, rewarding relationship—requires a deep understanding of the context in which our products and services are used in the course of our customers' day-to-day lives. Put simply, it requires a comprehensive view of consumer behavior. And the foundations of our marketing work— our Western analytic research methods—are simply not capable of providing that view. They have set us up to fail, time and again.

Consider for a moment how we measure the capstone of relationship marketing: customer satisfaction. Is it simply a question of expectations versus actual performance on a given attribute of a product or service? Is it a static, context-free rating on a five-point scale? The stories of consumers on the edge suggest that they aren't simply pleased or displeased with their computers, their answering machines, their trips to the grocery store. They are satisfied or dissatisfied with the quality of their lives in today's world. For contemporary consumers, *product* satisfaction is linked inextricably with *life* satisfaction, and companies must attend to both these dimensions if they expect to win.

Let's face it: problem-focused research studies and runaway numbers crunching are misleading. They are not designed to reveal the kind of consumer discontent we're describing; and in fact, they may get in the way of such insights. Isolated ratings of the sugar content in cereal or the readability of digital displays tell us nothing about despairing consumers and the role that marketing policies play in exacerbating their discontent. To get inside people's heads, marketers need to turn to the tools of ethnography and phenomenology: qualitative social-science methods dedicated to richly describing and interpreting people's lives. Videotapes and photography also are good reporting tools. They can reveal what a "day in the life of the customer" is all about. Finally, long-term studies work better than ad hoc surveys in painting an accurate picture of how consumers react to and use products.

We also can tap into underutilized data scattered within organizations to develop a more complete and intimate picture of consumers. Customer-service hot lines, for example, are a source of great insight, but few companies use them for that purpose. Ironically, many have outsourced their 800-number services and customer-response hot lines in the wake of cost cutbacks. Another underutilized resource is the World Wide Web. Because marketers do not directly maintain or intervene in product discussion groups, the conversations that develop there are especially revealing. Managers at Intel learned quickly—but not quickly enough—about the role played by discussion groups in fueling marketplace crises such as the one the company experienced with the Pentium processor. Soap opera writers regularly monitor viewers' reactions to evolving story lines, changing characters and plots in response to the voiced concerns of viewers. Middleburg Interactive Communications in New York has launched a new service called M-3 to serve this very need. M-3 scans the Internet daily for consumer discourse about companies and their brands and then offers its clients advice on how to respond.

There also are many readily available sources of relevant information outside companies. For example, more formal use could be made of trend analyses, such as those offered by the Yankelovich Monitor, Roper Reports, and the Public Pulse. These services provide cutting-edge indicators of shifts in the consumer psyche.

Ad agencies also are likely purveyors of trend information. And there's the recently formed International Society for Quality-of-Life Studies, which sponsors annual conferences and publications. Secondary data are another overlooked source of valuable information about consumers. We should be reading our target groups' magazines, watching their television shows, learning what issues dominate their fields of vision, and tracking how those concerns evolve and change over time.

Understanding the consumer will above all require us to get out into the field. And that doesn't just mean the researchers. It means senior managers, middle-level managers, engineers. If the target customer that a Kraft Foods manager is pursuing is the so-called middle-American mom, that manager should rent a van, drive her team to DeSoto, Missouri, and "live with the natives." She should go to church with them, hang out at the local VFW, attend the parent-teacher conference on Thursday night. One of the authors of this article did just that when working for Young and Rubican Advertising. Ten years later, video reports from that field-based research on the "new traditional woman" still inform creatives' opinions about the real consumers of Jell-O and other classic mainstream brands. Perhaps it's time we take the philosophy of "customer visits" embraced in business-to-business marketing into the customer domain.

To be truly effective, however, these methods require grounding in a strong disciplinary base of theory. Simple mastery of methods—long the kingpin of power in a data-intensive world—will no longer suffice. Understanding consumers' experience means embracing theories of philosophy, communications, counseling, psychology, and religious studies. Even such disciplines as medicine, law, and literature have a lot to offer. Each can give us a new, broad perspective on the emotional lives of our consumers and help us get past the narrow views that training has inured us to.

We can't do all this without redressing the role of marketing research. If researchers were truly the consumer specialists we intend them to be, primarily responsible for understanding their customer—mainstream Americans, technophobes, or whatever segmentation is deemed relevant—we would no longer think of them as tacticians, reporters, data crunchers, or facilitators of focus groups on a company's latest ad campaigns. Instead, they would be *strategic specialists* with a mandate to develop and communicate throughout the company an empathetic understanding of target consumers. The researcher would serve as kingpin of the entire relationship-marketing function, ensuring that the consumer was represented accurately and responsibly in the company's value creation and delivery processes.

Relationship marketing as it is currently practiced has not brought us closer to customers. It has sent us farther afield.

In the 1980s, advertising-agency account planners and qualitative research consultants performed the task of consumer specialists. Clients didn't have time for such basic research, what with all the scanner data there were to process and all the new-product concepts there were to screen. With downsizing, cutbacks, and identity crises within the discipline, there was no one left inside the company to assume these responsibilities anyway. But is this a function we want farmed out? If ever there was a capacity that must be served within the organization, this is it. This is where the consumer intermediary function is performed. This is, in effect, the foundation of the entire marketing discipline.

Marketers serve as the boundary between the consumer and the company. And in that capacity, they are both representatives of the company and advocates for the customer's point of view. Both roles are critical; and yet in recent years, the balance has become selfishly skewed. Relationship marketing as it is currently practiced has not brought us closer to our customers. Instead, it has sent us further afield. Our misguided actions have sparked a consumer backlash that endangers the reputation of relationship marketing, calling into question the viability of the entire marketing discipline going forward.

Relationship marketing can work if it delivers on the principles on which it was founded. It's startling how wrong we've been about what it takes to cultivate intimate relationships with customers. And it is alarming how quickly and thoughtlessly relationships can be destroyed through the muddled actions we often engage in. We've taken advantage of the words for long enough. It's time to think about—and act on—what being a partner in a relationship really means.

Originally published in January–February 1998
Reprint 98106

See Your Brands Through Your Customers' Eyes

CHRIS LEDERER AND SAM HILL

Executive Summary

SUBARU MARKETS an L.L. Bean Outback station wagon.
Dell stamps Microsoft and Intel logos on its computers.
Such interweaving of different companies' brands is now
commonplace. But one of the central tools of brand
management—portfolio mapping—has not kept pace with
changes in the marketplace. Most conventional brand
maps include only those brands owned by a company,
arranged along organizational lines with little regard for
how the brands influence the customer perceptions. In
this article, the authors present a new mapping tool—the
brand portfolio molecule—that reveals the way brands
appear to customers. The brand portfolio molecule
includes all the brands that factor into a consumer's decision to buy, whether or not the company owns them.

The first step in creating a brand portfolio molecule is
to determine which brands should or should not be

151

included. The second step is to classify each brand by asking five key questions: 1) How important is this brand to customers' purchase decisions about the brand you're mapping? 2) Is its influence positive or negative? 3) What market position does this brand occupy relative to the other brands in the portfolio? 4) How does this brand connect to the other brands in the portfolio? 5) How much control do you have over this brand? The last step is to map the molecule using a 3-D modeling program or by hand with pen and paper. Individual brands take the form of atoms, and they're clustered in ways that reflect how customers see them. The usefulness of the tool lies in its ability to show the many forces that influence a customer's buying decision—and to provide a powerful new way to think about brand strategy.

VOLKSWAGEN AND TREK team up to bundle bicycles with cars. American Airlines, Citibank, and Visa jointly offer a credit card. Subaru markets an L.L. Bean edition of its Outback station wagon. Dell stamps Microsoft and Intel logos on its computers. Toys R Us partners with Amazon.com to launch an on-line toy store.

The interweaving of brands, now commonplace in business, is changing the rules of brand management. Back when most brands succeeded or failed on their own merits—the quality of the products or services they represented, their positioning in the marketplace, the appeal of their advertising campaigns—it was sufficient to manage them as stand-alone entities. Today, brand management is considerably more complicated. It requires close attention to the often complex intersections between the brands of different companies. Do

Volkswagen's marketers have to keep Trek in mind when they're making a decision about the VW brand? Absolutely. Does L.L. Bean have to keep an eye on Subaru? You bet.

Yet we contend that one of the central tools of brand management—portfolio mapping—has not kept pace with changes in the marketplace. It still reflects two outdated assumptions: that companies need to concentrate only on their own brands and that each brand manager works on one brand at a time. A traditional brand map arranges a company's brands along organizational lines, with little regard to how the brands influence customer perceptions and with no regard to how they connect with brands of other companies. We believe it's high time that marketers abandoned this old approach. What's needed is an entirely new mapping tool that reflects the way brands actually appear to customers. In this article, we'll describe such a tool and show how it can be used to create multidimensional maps—we call them *brand portfolio molecules*—that reveal the relationships among diverse brands and provide a powerful new way to think about brand strategy.

We include in a company's portfolio all the brands that factor into a consumer's decision to buy, whether or not the company owns them.

Portfolios Redefined

A great deal has been written about managing brand portfolios in recent years. You're probably familiar with a lot of the jargon: ingredient brands, flanker brands, brand extensions, and so on. Such terms have served a useful purpose. They've helped companies think through the different roles played by the brands they own. Today, however, they can do more harm than good. Why? Because they impose an inwardly focused, company-centric view of a brand portfolio—a view that's out of sync with the realities of the market.

We use a much broader definition of brand portfolio. We include in a company's portfolio all the brands that factor into a consumer's decision to buy, whether or not the company owns them. Dell's brand portfolio, for example, would include Pentium and Windows. Citibank's would include American Airlines. (We use the term *brand system* to refer to all the brands a company owns.) In many cases, moreover, a portfolio should not include every brand a company owns. Take Unilever's Dove and Lever 2000 soap brands. Research indicates that to a Dove customer, the Lever 2000 brand is irrelevant; it exerts no influence over the buying decision. As a result, Lever 2000 should be excluded from the Dove portfolio.

When you think about brand portfolios in this new way, the traditional approach to brand mapping falls apart. A conventional map arranges all of a company's brands into a simple hierarchy, with the corporate brand at the top. A traditional brand map for Philip Morris, for example, would show the Philip Morris brand as an umbrella over the divisional brands—Miller, Kraft, and so forth. Each divisional brand in turn serves as an umbrella over individual product or product-category brands. Kraft, for instance, is over Maxwell House, which is over Maxwell House Master Blend. The advantage of such a hierarchy is that it allows all the brands owned by a company to be shown on a single page. The disadvantage is that it reflects the view from inside, emphasizing the reporting relationships of brand managers in the organization. It ignores the customer.

So how can you put the buyer's point of view first, while still retaining some semblance of organizational order? The answer lies in a 360-degree perspective—one that reflects both the workings of the internal organization and the perceptions of the external marketplace. Brand mapping, in other words, needs to become three-dimensional.

The Brand Portfolio Molecule

That brings us to the brand portfolio molecule. In a molecule map, individual brands take the form of atoms, and they're clustered in ways that reflect how customers see them. Take a look at the exhibit "The Miller High Life Brand Molecule." Miller High Life is one of the many beer brands sold by Philip Morris's Miller Brewing subsidiary, and this molecule indicates the complex relationships it has with other Miller brands as well as with the brands of other companies. We'll use this example to explain the elements of a portfolio molecule.

The first thing you notice is that the centermost atom is not the High Life brand but the general Miller brand. That's because beer drinkers' impressions of High Life are determined more by the general Miller name than by the High Life brand itself. In any molecule, the central atom is always the most influential brand—what we call the *lead brand*—whether it's the brand being mapped or not. Note also the wide assortment of brands included in the molecule. Some, like Miller Genuine Draft and Miller Lite, are other Miller brands. But then there are the brands of organizations that Miller sponsors, like NASCAR and the NFL, which also influence the way consumers view the High Life brand. We even include Blind Date, a series of rock concerts promoted by Miller Genuine Draft, because of the influence it's had over young

The Miller High Life Brand Molecule

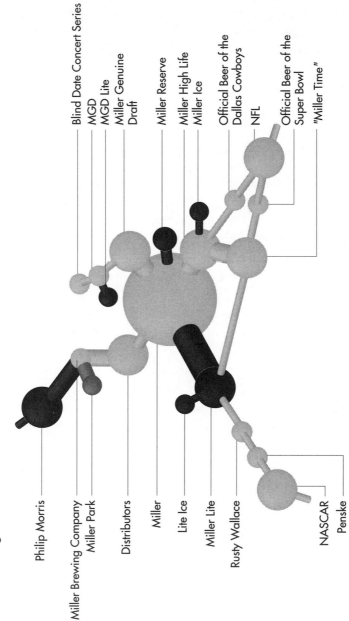

Blind Date Concert Series

MGD
MGD Lite
Miller Genuine Draft

Miller Reserve

Miller High Life
Miller Ice

Official Beer of the Dallas Cowboys

NFL

Official Beer of the Super Bowl

"Miller Time"

Philip Morris

Miller Brewing Company
Miller Park

Distributors

Miller

Lite Ice

Miller Lite

Rusty Wallace

NASCAR
Penske

people's perceptions of the Miller name. We don't include most other Philip Morris brands, like Kraft or Marlboro, as they have little or no impact on the decisions of beer buyers.

We use the size, shade, and location of atoms to indicate different characteristics of brands. Size represents role. The largest atom in the portfolio is the lead brand. Midsize atoms are *strategic brands*. They exert a strong influence over buyers, either blocking competitors from poaching current customers (as the slogan "Miller Time" does for High Life) or luring new users to the product (as Miller Genuine Draft does). The smallest atoms in the portfolio are *support brands*—they can help seal the deal with customers. The Dallas Cowboys and the Super Bowl, both of which Miller sponsors, play supporting roles for High Life. Atoms of any size that have open links as well as links to other atoms are *nodes*. These brands provide connections to other portfolios. In the High Life example, Philip Morris, NASCAR, and the NFL are nodes.

Shade indicates whether the brand exerts a positive influence (light), a negative influence (dark), or a neutral influence (medium) on the customer's buying decision. In the High Life molecule, the slogan "Miller Time" is light because it has created a strong sense of community among High Life drinkers. Miller Lite, on the other hand, is dark because it tends to undermine High Life's appeal to drinkers of heartier beers. Miller Park, the baseball stadium of the Milwaukee Brewers, has a neutral influence and thus is medium. Brands are considered neutral when buyers are aware of them but have not developed strong feelings, either positive or negative, toward them.

Location has two facets. First is proximity, which indicates the relatedness of market positionings. Miller

Genuine Draft and Miller Reserve are both near High
Life, indicating similar positionings (and a potential for
confusing customers). Miller Lite is farther away, indicating a more distinct positioning. The second facet of
location is linkage. Links between atoms indicate the
company's relationship to the brands. A single link, like
that between Miller and Miller Lite, shows that a Miller
manager has a direct relationship with Lite. A string of
links shows an indirect relationship, like that between a
Miller manager and the NFL. The width of the link indicates degree of control. The thicker the link, the easier it
is for Miller's managers to wield control over that brand.
While High Life's brand team can, for example, exert significant influence over Miller Genuine Draft, a sister
brand, it has much less influence over NASCAR, an outside partner with many other sponsors.

No doubt, there is quite a bit going on in a brand portfolio molecule. But that's as it should be. After all, there's
a lot going on in the marketplace that influences the
choices customers make. The usefulness of the molecule
tool lies in its ability to show all these forces in a clear,
graphical way.

Creating a Brand Molecule

Let's look at the three steps involved in creating a brand
molecule: taking inventory of the brands that influence
customers' perceptions and choices, classifying those
brands, and mapping the molecule. As an example, we'll
walk through the process as it might play out for General
Motors' Cadillac brand, and we'll show how the resulting
molecule sheds new light on Cadillac's brand strategy.
Several years ago, we worked extensively with the Cadil-

lac marketing team, and our interest in the challenges facing the brand comes from that work. What we say here, however, is based on a more recent, independent analysis of Cadillac, for which we interviewed luxury car buyers and drew on publicly available data. It represents solely our views on Cadillac's brand strategy.

TAKING INVENTORY

Determining which brands should or should not be included in a molecule takes a fair bit of digging—several weeks of effort are usually involved. You can't just grab information off a trademark list from the U.S. Patent and Trademark Office. Trademark lists often contain lots of duplications, and they seldom include the names of important marketing partners. Instead, you have to undertake a broad brainstorming effort, asking managers from across your organization—R&D, manufacturing, promotions, sales—to list any brands they feel should be considered for the portfolio. Existing market research—quantitative brand-tracking studies, focus groups, home use tests, and so on—can also be a valuable source of information. The intent at the outset is to be as inclusive as possible; you don't want to overlook potentially critical brands.

The master list of brands then has to be pruned down to those that have a demonstrated impact on customers' buying decisions. Again, existing market research can be valuable. Data on customer awareness, purchase intent, and switching behavior can provide an initial screen. But don't expect to get all the answers from available data. You'll probably need to gather additional information. We've found that focus groups and on-line quantitative surveys can often help fill in the data gaps. Whatever you do, don't rush through this step. It should be a highly iterative process with many rounds of discussion and analysis.

In thinking about the brands that influence the potential Cadillac buyer, at least a dozen familiar names come to mind, including General Motors, Cadillac itself, the nickname "Caddie," and the various Cadillac sub-brands, such as Seville, DeVille, Eldorado, and Catera. Less well-known but nonetheless influential brands include concept cars such as the Steinmetz Catera, engineered by Steinmetz-Opel in Germany, and Evoq, designed by Cadillac.

The array of branded features used in Cadillac cars must also be considered. Brands that GM or Cadillac owns, such as OnStar, StabiliTrak, Magnasteer, Twilight Sentinel, PASS-Key II, and Zebrano wood, make the cut, as well as brands owned by suppliers, such as Bose sound systems, Bosch brakes, and Michelin tires.

That's not all. New York's Potamkin dealership deploys a substantial marketing budget of its own. Put it in as a proxy for all dealers? Of course. The Senior PGA Golf Tour, which Cadillac sponsors, is another relevant brand. Cadillac is the "official car" of Pebble Beach, so the golf resort goes on the list, too. And we can't forget the ghosts of Cadillac past. Remember, if consumers consider a brand as part of their purchase decisions, that brand belongs in the molecule, whether or not the company controls the brand and whether or not the brand still exists in the market. The Fleetwood, the Cimarron, and the Allante—all discontinued Cadillac models that continue to influence customer impressions—belong on the list. We'd even argue for the inclusion of Elvis Presley, perhaps the most famous owner of Cadillacs.

The exhibit "A First Cut at the Cadillac Brand Inventory" shows the final list of relevant brands, arranged according to traditional brand-management categories. We find it best to start with traditional categories, as they're the ones brand teams are most familiar with. In the next step, we'll reclassify the brands into more meaningful categories.

CLASSIFYING

Once you have a well-vetted list of brands, you need to classify each one as lead, strategic, or support; gauge the kind and degree of influence it exerts; and determine its relative market positioning. To do so, ask yourself five questions:

- How important is this brand to customers' purchase decisions about the brand being mapped?

- Is its influence positive or negative?

- What market position does this brand occupy relative to the other brands in the portfolio?

- How does this brand connect to the other brands in the portfolio?

- How much control do you have over this brand?

You may already have the answers to many of these questions, thanks to the data you reviewed and the thinking you did in completing the inventory. (Indeed, much of the classification can usually be done at the inventory stage.) Rank-order purchase intent data, for example, help define a brand's role; switching data can provide insight into influence; promotional pieces like print ads and mail inserts can help with connection; and

A First Cut at the Cadillac Brand Inventory

Taking inventory is the first step in creating a brand portfolio molecule. The list of relevant brands in the Cadillac brand portfolio is arranged here according to traditional brand-management categories.

	Owned	Not Owned
Endorser	General Motors	
Master	Cadillac	Bosch
	Caddie	Bose
		Elvis Presley
		EWGA
		Le Mans Racing
		Michelin
		PGA
		Pebble Beach
		Potamkin (etc.)
		Senior PGA Tour
		Toyota
Line	Allante	
	Catera	
	Cimarron	
	DeVille	
	Eldorado	
	Escalade	
	Fleetwood	
	Seville	
	Team Cadillac	
Product	DHS	
	DTS	
	Evoq	
	SLS	
	STS	
Ingredient	Magnasteer	
	Night Vision	
	Northstar	
	OnStar	
	PASS-Key II	
	StabiliTrak	
	Steinmetz-Opel	
	Twilight Sentinel	
	Zebrano Wood	

organization charts and trademark ownership lists can help determine level of control. Inevitably, though, you'll need to make some judgment calls. Don't be afraid to trust your team's wisdom, but try to keep purely subjective judgments to a minimum.

In classifying the Cadillac portfolio, we start by determining the lead brand. In this case (unlike in the Miller High Life case), our interviews with potential customers show that the Cadillac name itself exerts the biggest influence over luxury car buyers. So Cadillac is the lead brand. We also draw heavily on customer research to classify the other brands. OnStar and Night Vision, both ingredient brands in the traditional hierarchy, are important factors in customers' purchases. Therefore, they're classified as strategic brands. General Motors, usually on top of the traditional brand hierarchy, falls to the bottom of our categorization. It does not play a big role in customers' decisions, so it's a support brand. The various subbrands also play different roles. STS, a model with a distinct and strong positioning to consumers, assumes a strategic position, while its less influential sister product, SLS, takes a support position. The classification proceeds in this way until all the brands are categorized.

To gauge influence, we asked Cadillac owners why they bought their cars. Branded features, like StabiliTrak and OnStar, were high on the list and thus get positive ratings. We determined positioning by asking customers to compare sets of brands. We found that Catera, for example, is seen as very different from traditional Cadillac models, with a positioning distinct from the lead brand. We reviewed public data and Web sites to uncover brand connections. We found that while Cadillac brand managers work directly with dealers like

Potamkin, they have indirect relationships with marketing partners like Le Mans Racing.

Determining the degree of control Cadillac has over each brand is fairly straightforward. Roughly one-third of the brands in the portfolio are controlled by the Cadillac brand management group. Cadillac has much less influence over branded features supplied by outside companies, such as Bose audio systems, which are often shared with many competing car companies. It also has limited influence over GM-owned features, which are often shared with sister divisions and even competitors. For example, OnStar is now available in other GM cars and will soon be offered in Toyota's U.S. models. Also, while Cadillac may exercise influence over dealers and the organizations it sponsors, it certainly does not control them.

The last step is to note which brands in the portfolio are nodes. For Cadillac, General Motors serves as a node to many other brand portfolios, such as Chevrolet and Buick, as does Potamkin, which sells other car lines. OnStar is also a node since it is available in other brands of cars.

By the end of the classification phase, you should have a spreadsheet or table that measures each brand across the five key dimensions: importance to purchase, influence on purchase, positioning, connections, and degree of control. We show such a chart for the Cadillac analysis in the exhibit "Data Table for the Cadillac Portfolio." From this analysis, we can reclassify the brand inventory according to role and degree of control, as shown in the exhibit "The Cadillac Brand Portfolio."

MAPPING THE MOLECULE

This step is the easiest. It's a matter of putting the data into a 3-D modeling program like Strata Studio Pro or

Academic MetaCreations Infini-D. (If you don't have such software, don't despair. You can map a molecule using pen and paper, as described in the exhibit "A Low-Tech Approach.") For a company with few brands, mapping should take one to five days. When we mapped the brand portfolio of Ping, the golf club manufacturer, it took about four days to plot the 57 brands involved. Bigger portfolios will take more time.

Mapping, it should be noted, is not a one-shot deal. The first draft should be viewed as just that: a draft. You need to present it to your brand team and encourage them to poke holes in it. Typically, the discussions will raise questions about the underlying classification. Don't be afraid to go back to the drawing board and refine the classification, even gathering new data if necessary. Expect to go through a number of versions. Always push to find new connections among brands, to debate the levels of control, and to question the relative importance assigned to each atom. These discussions, as much as the resulting map, will help you challenge your marketing assumptions and gain new insight into your brand strategy.

For instance, if you realize that two equally important strategic brands lie in very different positions, you may want to split the portfolio into two separate portfolios—we call that tactic "partitioning" the molecule. The two portfolios should be managed separately, to maintain their distinctiveness to customers. On the other hand, a molecule that has two or more strategic brands in close proximity may indicate a need to combine brands. Miller, for example, may want to think hard about maintaining High Life, Genuine Draft, and Reserve as separate brands. (A molecule's ability to display brand overlaps can be particularly valuable in the wake of a merger.) In constructing a molecule, you can

Data Table for the Cadillac Portfolio

To create the data table, make a numbered list of all brands in the inventory. Based on your answers to the questions in the classification phase, assign numeric values for each brand along the five dimensions as follows:

Importance (size): lead brand = 2.0, strategic = 1.5, support = 1.0; Influence (shade): positive = 1.0, negative = -1.0, neutral = 0; Positioning (location): coordinates on the axes reflect market positioning—those brands with similar positionings are assigned coordinates close to one another; those with distinct positionings receive coordinates in separate quadrants; Connections (links): for each brand, indicate which of the other brands connect to it by marking their list number(s); Degree of control (thickness of links): high = 75%, medium = 50%, low = 25%, 0% = none

Brand Role	Brand	Importance	Influence	POSITIONING			Connections	Degree of Control (%)
				X	Y	Z		
Lead	1 Cadillac	2.0	0	0	0	0		
Strategic	2 Caddie	1.5	0	0.5	0.5	0	1	75
	3 Catera	1.5	1	2	2	0	2	75
	4 Eldorado	1.5	-1	-0.5	0.5	0	1	75
	5 Elvis Presley	1.5	1	-1.5	2	0		0
	6 Escalade	1.5	0	1	-0.5	-0.5	1	75
	7 Evoq	1.5	1	2	0	-2	1	50
	8 Night Vision	1.5	1	-1	-2	1	1	25
	9 Northstar	1.5	1	-1.5	-1	1	1	25
	10 OnStar	1.5	1	-2	-1	0	1	25
	11 Potamkin (etc.)	1.5	1	-2.5	2	-1	1	50
	12 Seville	1.5	0	0.5	0	-0.5	1	75

Support

	C1	C2	C3	C4	C5	C6	C7
13 StabiliTrak	1.5	1	-0.5	0	0	1	50
14 STS	1.5	1	1.5	0	-0.5	12	75
15 Allante	1.0	-1	-0.5	2	0.5	1	25
16 Bosch	1.0	1	-2	0	-0.5	1	25
17 Bose	1.0	1	-2	0	0	1	25
18 Cimarron	1.0	-1	-0.5	2	-0.5	1	25
19 DeVille	1.0	-1	0.5	1	-0.5	1	75
20 DHS	1.0	-1	0.5	1.5	-0.5	19	75
21 DTS	1.0	-1	0.5	1.5	-0.5	19	75
22 EWGA	1.0	1	0.5	-2	-0.5	1	25
23 Fleetwood	1.0	-1	-0.5	2	-1	1	25
24 General Motors	1.0	-1	-1.5	-2	1	1, 8, 9, 10, 26, 28, 36, 37	25
25 Le Mans Racing	1.0	1	2.5	0	-2	7	25
26 Magnasteer	1.0	0	-1	0	0	1	25
27 Michelin	1.0	1	-2	0	0.5	1	25
28 PASS-Key II	1.0	0	0	-2	-1	1	25
29 Pebble Beach	1.0	1	1	-2	0.5	1	25
30 PGA	1.0	1	2	-2	0.5	31	25
31 Senior PGA Tour	1.0	0	1.5	-2	0.5	34	25
32 SLS	1.0	-1	1	0	-0.5	12	75
33 Steinmetz-Opel	1.0	1	2	2.5	0	3	25
34 Team Cadillac	1.0	0	1	-2	0.5	1	50
35 Toyota	1.0	-1	-2.5	-1	0	10	25
36 Twilight Sentinel	1.0	0	-1	-1	-1	1	25
37 Zebrano Wood	1.0	0	0	-2	0	1	25

The Cadillac Brand Portfolio

*The Cadillac brand inventory is reclassified above according to role
(how important each brand is to the customer's decision to buy) and
degree of control (how much influence Cadillac's brand managers have
over each brand).*

	DEGREE OF CONTROL		
	High	**Medium**	**Low**
Lead	Cadillac		
Strategic	Caddie	Evoq	Elvis Presley
	Catera	Potamkin (etc.)	Night Vision
	Eldorado	StabiliTrak	Northstar
	Escalade		OnStar
	Seville		
	STS		
Support	DeVille	Team Cadillac	Allante
	DHS		Bosch
	DTS		Bose
	SLS		Cimarron
			EWGA
			Fleetwood
			General Motors
			Le Mans Racing
			Magnasteer
			Michelin
			PASS-Key II
			Pebble Beach
			PGA
			Senior PGA Tour
			Steinmetz-Opel
			Toyota
			Twilight Sentinel
			Zebrano Wood

A Low-Tech Approach

Although we recommend using 3-D modeling software to map brand molecules, it is possible to draw them by hand or with a word-processing program. This chart shows how the Miller High Life molecule would look using a low-tech approach. The size and shade of the typeface indicate each brand's role and influence. Shade indicates whether the brand exerts a positive influence (dark), a negative influence (medium), or a neutral influence (light), on the customers' buying decision. The length and width of connecting lines indicate positioning and degree of control. All the information in a 3-D molecule can be captured in the hand-drawn version, though brand relationships are less dramatically portrayed.

also identify opportunities for brand extensions (where holes exist), umbrella brands (where clusters exist), and other branding tactics that can increase the effectiveness and efficiency of your marketing.

Interpreting the Cadillac Molecule

The Cadillac molecule is shown in the exhibit "A Molecular View of the Cadillac Brand." So what does it tell us? To answer that question, we need first to briefly review Cadillac's existing brand strategy. For much of the twentieth century, Cadillac dominated the U.S. luxury car market. As recently as 1994, it sold 210,686 cars, accounting for a market share of more than 30%. However, Cadillac has since slipped precipitously. Its customer base has aged, and it has been unable to attract younger buyers to its brands, as competitors like Mercedes and BMW have. By 1999, Cadillac had slid to third in the luxury car rankings, behind Mercedes and Lexus, with Lincoln and BMW close behind. In a market that grew 50% over that time span, Cadillac's volume shrank by 15%. Its market share was down to just over 17%.

At the moment, Cadillac's brand strategy appears to focus on using product subbrands to attract two very different sorts of buyers. It is using the slicker Seville STS and Catera models to bring in new, younger customers while using Eldorado and DeVille to retain older, more traditional customers. It has revamped its advertising to make the overall image of the brand more youthful; the campaign emphasizes the cutting edge technology embedded in the vehicles, as represented by branded features like OnStar and Night Vision. And, to encourage greater innovation and responsiveness among its employees,

The image of Cadillac continues to be shaped by brands that are tied to the company's past and to its older, traditional customers—and that directly contradicts Cadillac's advertising strategy.

A Molecular View of the Cadillac Brand

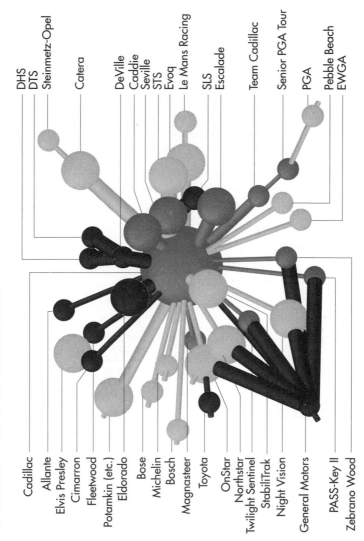

DHS
DTS
Steinmetz-Opel

Catera

DeVille
Caddie
Seville
STS
Evoq
Le Mans Racing

SLS
Escalade

Team Cadillac

Senior PGA Tour

PGA

Pebble Beach
EWGA

Cadillac
Allante
Elvis Presley
Cimarron
Fleetwood
Potamkin (etc.)
Eldorado

Bose
Michelin
Bosch

Magnasteer

Toyota

OnStar
Northstar
Twilight Sentinel
StabiliTrak
Night Vision

General Motors

PASS-Key II
Zebrano Wood

Cadillac has put in place a new organizational structure for the brand, with separate marketing managers and budgets for each major car line.

Despite the intensity of the efforts, the Cadillac brand continues to decline. We think the brand molecule indicates why. It shows that the major thrusts of the company's brand strategy are flawed. First, and most obviously, the company's image is mainly set by the Cadillac brand itself; trying to change that image by promoting product subbrands probably won't work. We can also immediately see that the old nickname "Caddie" continues to bear an intense relationship to Cadillac—Caddie lies virtually on top of the Cadillac brand. DeVille, for most consumers, is also almost synonymous with Cadillac and thus lies close to the Cadillac sphere. The image of Cadillac, in other words, continues to be shaped by brands that are tied to the company's past and to its older, traditional customers—and that directly contradicts the company's advertising strategy. Unless Cadillac decides to kill these brands, or at least avoid advertising them, it will have a tough time changing its image.

In contrast to the older brands, Catera lies much farther away from the Cadillac lead brand. That's a direct result of the division's attempt to position that car to be distinct from the main brand—clearly, a case where a product marketing strategy undermines the broader brand strategy. Intended as a silver-bullet brand that would attract younger customers to the Cadillac brand, Catera is unlikely to fulfill that mission. It may well be a successful car, if judged on its own, but it simply lacks the influence over customers to make a measurable impact on perceptions of Cadillac. A silver-bullet brand might indeed be a solution for Cadillac, but it would have to be positioned much closer to the lead brand—in the way that Apple positioned the iMac near the Macintosh brand.

The money spent to hype high-tech features like OnStar and Northstar could, moreover, backfire. Because these brands are shared with other automobile lines that often have very different market positions (think of Toyota), they could distort perceptions of the Cadillac brand.

Put bluntly, a brand manager, using the molecule approach, might well reverse virtually every aspect of recent Cadillac strategy. That's what can happen when you see your brands as your customers do.

Originally published in June 2001
Reprint R0106J

About the Contributors

LEONARD L. BERRY is Distinguished Professor of Marketing and holds the M.B. Zale Chair in Retailing and Marketing Leadership in the Lowry Mays College of Business at Texas A&M University. He is the founder of Texas A&M's Center for Retailing Studies and served as its Director for eighteen years. He also is a Former National President of the American Marketing Association, and is currently a member of the board of directors of several major public companies. He is the author of numerous books including *Discovering the Soul of Service* and *On Great Service.*

RICHARD B. CHASE is the Justin B. Dart Professor of Operations Management at the University of Southern California Marshall School of Business. An admitted service junkie, some of his recent articles include "The Ten Commandments of E-service," "Make Your Service Fail-safe" (with Doug Stewart), "The Strategic Levers of Yield Management" (with Sheryl Kimes), and "How Do Financial Services Stack-up? Findings from a Benchmarking Study of the U.S. Financial Service Sector" (with Aleda Roth and Chris Voss). He is currently coauthoring a book with Sriram Dasu entitled *The Science of Service*, which translates scientific findings from behavioral science into guidelines for service design and improvement. His e-mail address is richard.chase@marshall.usc.edu.

SRIRAM DASU is Associate Professor of Operations Management at the University of Southern California Marshall School of Business. He has published several articles on supply chain management and service operations management. Some of his articles include "Optimizing an International Network of Plants," "Nature of Service Recovery Expectations," and "A Dynamic Process Model of Dissatisfaction for Unfavorable, Non-routine Service Encounters." He is currently coauthoring a book with Richard Chase entitled *The Science of Service*, which translates scientific findings from behavioral science into guidelines for service design and improvement. His e-mail address is Sriram.dasu@marshall.usc.edu.

SUSAN DOBSCHA is Associate Professor of Marketing at Bentley College. Her research interests include consumer resistance to marketing tactics, gender and consumer culture, and eco-feminist theory applied to social issues such as consumerism. Her teaching credits include consumer behavior, marketing research, and green marketing.

SUSAN FOURNIER is an Associate Professor of Business Administration in the Marketing area at the Harvard Business School. At HBS, Professor Fournier teaches the Brand Marketing M.B.A. elective and is Director of the *Managing Brand Meanings* Executive Education Program. Her research examines the types of relationships consumers form with brands, the strength and durability of those relationships (as measured by her Brand Relationship Quality scale), and the ways that marketer actions enhance and dilute consumer-brand bonds. She applies her relationship frameworks to better understand brand loyalty, brand equity, brand personality, and customer satisfaction, especially within packaged good and technological product domains. Professor Fournier's work has been published in numerous journals, including *Journal of Consumer Research, Journal of Marketing,* and *Har-*

vard Business Review, and has been referenced in periodicals such as *The Economist*, the *New York Times*, and *U.S. News & World Report*. Prior to joining HBS, Professor Fournier served as vice president and associate research director at Young & Rubicam New York. She also held positions as New Product Forecasting Analyst at Yankelovich, Clancy, Schulman and Advertising Research Manager at Polaroid Corporation. Professor Fournier currently consults with a range of consumer marketing companies, advertising agencies, law firms, and research firms in the area of brand relationship management, including Coca-Cola, Intel, McKinsey & Company, Saatchi and Saatchi Advertising, and VISA USA. Professor Fournier also serves on the editorial boards of several journals, and is on the boards of advisors for Crave Technologies, Inc., and Invivia, Inc., both Web-based service organizations.

As President of Helios Consulting, SAM HILL works with senior executives at a number of *Fortune* 500 companies on growth strategy, marketing, and brands. Mr. Hill's work has appeared in *Strategy & Business*, *Estrategia & Negocios*, *The Financial Times*, and *The Wall Street Journal* and has been featured in *Business 2.0*, *Harvard Business Review*, *Salon*, and the *New York Times*. He is also a columnist for *Fortune Small Business Magazine*, and is the author of two books: *Radical Marketing*, which was named one of *Fortune*'s Best Business Books of 1999, and *The Infinite Asset*, coauthored with Chris Lederer. Before cofounding Helios, Mr. Hill was Vice Chairman and Chief Strategic Officer in New York at D'Arcy, the world's twelfth largest advertising agency, and Chief Marketing Officer and Lead Partner at Booz·Allen & Hamilton in Chicago and Sydney. He began his career at Kraft General Foods as an engineer and later served as Director of International Strategy. Mr. Hill speaks to ten thousand executives at twenty-five major forums in seven countries annually.

JON R. KATZENBACH is Senior Partner of Katzenbach Partners LLC, a consulting firm in New York City that specializes in leadership, team, and workforce performance. He is the author of *Teams at the Top* and coauthor of *Real Change Leaders*, as well as of the bestseller *The Wisdom of Teams*. His most recent book, *Peak Performance*, describes how the twenty-five top performing companies obtain emotional commitment from their workforce.

CHRIS LEDERER is Cofounder of Helios Consulting Group in New York City. Mr. Lederer consults with senior executives on their most pressing growth issues. His particular areas of expertise are optimizing complex brand portfolios and e-branding. Prior to Helios, Mr. Lederer was in the Marketing Intensive Industries Practice at Booz·Allen & Hamilton, where he worked on growth-related problems for clients, primarily in media and entertainment industries. Before that, Mr. Lederer spent seven years obtaining classical sales and marketing skills as a Fast Track Professional Development Sales Manager at RJR/Nabisco, an Account Supervisor at North Castle Advertising, and a Brand Manager at Lever Brothers. Brands that he had direct involvement with during this time included LifeSavers, Wisk, and Lever 2000. His first book, *The Infinite Asset*, will be published in September 2001. He is currently a board member of eCompanystore.com.

DAVID GLEN MICK is the Robert Hill Carter Professor of Commerce at the McIntire School of Commerce at the University of Virginia and an Adjunct Professor of Administrative Medicine in the Medical School at the University of Wisconsin-Madison. He has previously served on the faculties of Indiana University, the University of Florida, the Copenhagen Business School, Dublin City University, and the University of Wisconsin-Madison. He has also served as Associate Editor and Editor of the *Journal of Consumer Research*. His research centers on the nature and role of meaning in consumer behavior, particularly in the domains of advertising, gift giving, and the consumption of technological products. His research has appeared in numerous outlets, including the *Journal of Consumer Research, Journal of Marketing, Harvard Business Review,* and *International Journal of Research in Marketing.* His writing has been acknowledged with many awards, most notably the 1999 Maynard Award for the most significant contribution to marketing theory and thought, a recognition for Best Article in the *Journal of Consumer Research* for 1986–1988, and two other notable recognitions from the Association for Consumer Research and the American Marketing Association. He has been invited to present his research at business schools and universities worldwide, including Oxford, the London Business School, the Stockholm School of Economics, Columbia, Duke, Harvard, and others.

C.K. PRAHALAD is the Harvey C. Fruehauf Professor of Business Administration at the University of Michigan Business School. His research focuses on the role and value of top management in large, diversified, multinational corporations, and he has consulted with numerous firms worldwide. Mr. Prahalad is the coauthor, with Gary Hamel, of *Competing for the Future,* named by *Business Week* as one of the year's best management books in 1994. He is also the author of many award-winning articles, such as "Strategic Intent" and "The Core Competence of the Corporation," which won McKinsey Prizes in 1989 and 1990, respectively.

VENKATRAM ("VENKAT") RAMASWAMY is a Professor of Marketing, Hallman Fellow of Electronic Business, and Director of the Center for Business Innovation, University of Michigan Business School. Dr. Ramaswamy addresses fundamental issues in the "new" economy, particularly the transformation of value and its creation, and its implications for innovation.

He is codeveloping "The Experience Revolution Community," a software innovation in knowledge creation enabled by the PRAJA platform.

JASON A. SANTAMARIA is an Investment Banking Associate at Morgan Stanley & Company in New York City and is a recent graduate of The University of Pennsylvania's Wharton School of Business. Prior to Wharton, Mr. Santamaria worked at McKinsey & Company as a Business Analyst, served as an artillery officer in the United States Marine Corps, and conducted research in Venezuela as a J. William Fulbright Scholar.

MOHANBIR SAWHNEY is the McCormick Tribune Professor of Electronic Commerce and Technology and the Chair of the Technology & e-Commerce Program at the Kellogg School of Management, Northwestern University. Professor Sawhney is a globally recognized author, teacher, speaker, and consultant in e-business strategy and technology marketing. He is the coauthor of two recent books: *The Seven Steps to Nirvana: Strategic Insights into eBusiness Transformation* and *Techventure: New Rules on Value and Profit from Silicon Valley*. His research has appeared in leading journals like *California Management Review, Harvard Business Review, Management Science, Marketing Science, Journal of Interactive Marketing*, and *Journal of the Academy of Marketing Science*. He also writes extensively for trade publications like *Financial Times, CIO Magazine, Context*, and *Business 2.0*. His speaking and consulting clients include dozens of *Fortune* 500 companies in over fifteen countries. He serves on the advisory boards of several early-stage technology companies. Professor Sawhney has received several teaching awards, including the Outstanding Professor of the Year at Kellogg in 1998 and the Sidney Levy Award for Excellence in Teaching in 1999 and 1995. He is a

Fellow of the World Economic Forum, a Fellow at Diamond-Cluster International, a member of Merrill Lynch's Tech-Brains Advisory Board, and a member of the NRI Advisory Committee on Telecom for the Government of India.

PATRICIA B. SEYBOLD is the Founder and CEO of the Patricia Seybold Group (www.psgroup.com), a worldwide research and consulting firm and the customer-centric executives' first choice for strategic insight, technology guidance, and e-business best practices. Founded in 1978 and based in Boston, Massachusetts, the firm offers customized consulting services, an online strategic research service, executive workshops, and in-depth research reports. Ms. Seybold is the author of *Customers.com*, a *Business Week, New York Times, Wall Street Journal*, and *USA Today* best-selling book. *Customers.com* offers insight into creating breakthrough practices in electronic commerce and asserts that successful e-businesses tend to be more customer-friendly. Ms. Seybold's latest book, *The Customer Revolution*, demonstrates how to measure and monitor what matters most to a company's customers.

Index